A DARING COIFFEUR
Reflections on *War and Peace* and *Anna Karenina*

By the same author

*

THE LAST SUMMER
(a novel)

A
DARING COIFFEUR

REFLECTIONS ON
War and Peace and *Anna Karenina*

By

ELIZABETH GUNN

1971
CHATTO & WINDUS
LONDON

Published by
Chatto and Windus Ltd
40/42 William IV Street
London WC2

*

Clarke, Irwin & Co Ltd
Toronto

ISBN 0 7011 1754 0

Printed in Great Britain by
T. & A. CONSTABLE LTD
Hopetoun Street, Edinburgh

CONTENTS

ERRATA

p. 41 line 11. Add quotation mark to read: 'The Countess . . .
lines 23-4. The quotation 'she would die . . . ' should
be within double quotation marks. A single quotation mark should close the paragraph.

p. 42 line 3 from foot of page
Add words to read: the Count angrily.'

p. 43 line 16. A colon should replace semi-colon.

p. 96 line 12. Insert 'not' to read: this did not occur to us.

'I remember in Gaspra he read Leo Shestov's book *Good and Evil in the Teaching of Nietzsche and Tolstoi*, and, when Anton Tchekov remarked that he did not like the book, Tolstoi said: "I thought it amusing. It's written swaggeringly, but it's all right and interesting. I'm sure I like cynics when they are sincere. Now he says: 'Truth is not wanted'; quite true, what should he want truth for? For he will die all the same. . . ." After lunch on the terrace, he took up the book again, and, finding the passage, "Tolstoi, Dostoevsky, Nietzsche could not live without an answer to their questions, and for them any answer was better than none," he laughed and said: "What a daring coiffeur; he says straight that I deceived myself, and that means that I deceived others too. That is the obvious conclusion. . . ." '

Reminiscences of Leo Nicolayevitch Tolstoi
by Maxim Gorky

ACKNOWLEDGMENTS

In the essay on WAR AND PEACE I have used Louise and Aylmer Maude's translation, Macmillan, London 1967.
In ANNA KARENINA I have principally used Rosemary Edmunds' translation, Penguin, London 1969; any departure from this is indicated in the text.

E. G.

ON WAR AND PEACE

'In every wrinkle, every muscle, in the breadth of these shoulders, the thickness of these legs in enormous boots: in every movement, quiet, firm and deliberate, are seen the distinctive traits of that which form the strength of the Russian—his simplicity and obstinacy.'

Sevastopol Sketches, p. 16,
translated by Aylmer and Louise Maude

IT IS possible to spend a lifetime re-reading this book without the slightest impulse to analyse. This alone is sufficient to provoke the question: 'Why?' The book itself presents a paradox, a dichotomy stranger, perhaps, than that of any novel. And yet—we do not even notice this.

Why then? The answer surely lies in the mood, the euphoria *War and Peace* engenders in its readers. This euphoric mood is itself anomalous. How is it that we can read about such things, intrigues in the death chamber, war, family partings, the cruelty of husbands to wives and fathers to daughters, the terrors of battle, its fears and its horrors, its corpses and mutilations, how is it that we can read of these things and smile? For we not only do smile and feel glad—Tolstoy invites us to do so. See p. 189: ' "Here it is dreadful but enjoyable", was what the face of each soldier and each officer seemed to say.' Tolstoy himself goes further: 'In the midst of the worst, perhaps then even most of all, it is a pleasure to be alive.'

Happiness is synonymous with intensity of living; it includes a sense of one's own strength, an irrational joy-fulness, one, that is, for which there is no apparent cause in circumstances. This is a recurrent, it might almost be called *the* theme of the first half of *War and Peace*. It

3

inspires both Prince Andrew's bitter outburst on p. 21 of the book in which he inveighs against 'drawing-rooms, gossip, balls, vanity and triviality . . .' and is perhaps most fully, explicitly developed on p. 151:

' "One step beyond that boundary line which resembles the line dividing the living from the dead, lies uncertainty, suffering and death. And what is there? Who is there?—there beyond that field, that tree, that roof lit up by the sun? No one knows, but one wants to know. You fear and yet long to cross that line, and know that sooner or later it must be crossed and you will have to find out what is there, just as you will inevitably have to learn what lies on the other side of death. But you are strong, healthy, cheerful, and excited, and are surrounded by other such excitedly animated and healthy men." So thinks, or at any rate feels, anyone who comes in sight of the enemy, and that feeling gives a particular glamour and *glad keenness of impression* [my italics] to everything that takes place at such a moment.'

In early life it is taken for granted that this is what happiness is. The conception rarely survives middle age. One of the reasons, perhaps, is illustrated by Tolstoy in Nicholas Rostov's horrified reaction when, wounded, he suddenly sees the enemy coming towards him: 'He looked at the approaching Frenchmen and though but a moment before he had been galloping to get at them and hack them to pieces, their proximity now seemed so awful that he could not believe his eyes. "Who are they? Why are they running? Can they be coming at me? And why? To kill *me*? Me whom everyone is so fond of?" He remembered his mother's love for him, and his family and

4

his friends and the enemy's intention to kill him seemed impossible. . . .' In other words when one is young one does not believe in one's own death. When one is older death becomes possible. One no longer welcomes danger if afraid of death—unless as a means of overcoming one's fear; and if one has lost this fear or come to terms with it one may no longer need to live intensely, or one may live intensely but more calmly so. And, indeed, as *War and Peace* goes on and the characters in it age the original torrent of joyfulness dries up. It carries us roughly half-way through, to the opening of Book IX, making later intermittent appearances, its last real appearance, fittingly perhaps, in the childlike hero Pierre Bezhukov, who, relieved of his rich man's existence with its aimlessness and luxury, suffering extreme deprivation 'felt a new strength and joy in life such as he had never before known. And this not only stayed with him during the whole of his imprisonment but even grew in strength as the hardships of his position increased.'

Is it then in search of happiness that men become soldiers and go to war and kill one another? Is this not a contradiction?—But then have we not said that happiness in Tolstoy is contradictory, is distinguished precisely by its tactless character? Natasha at her parents' dinner-party standing up, aged thirteen, and asking, as she has been dared to do, in clear bell-like tones, what is for pudding—does not Natasha at this moment seem herself to sum up, to personify Tolstoy's conception of happiness? And we cannot ourselves help feeling it to be a true conception; happiness cannot be pre-arranged or planned; we cannot even rely on being happy when we ought to be so, when we have attained what we desired, when there is every reason for happiness; this is one of the chief causes of unhappiness.

Going on leave Nicholas Rostov cannot wait to be home. He urges on the coachman, and runs up the stairs. And his happiness, everyone's happiness, is just as he had pictured it. Despite this he very quickly grows bored. Inactive, he is restless. He cannot avoid the feeling that the happiness is less than it should have been.

It is not only happiness, however, that Tolstoy portrays as a tease, as lacking a proper sense of time and place. Nothing is as it should be (if it is, it is false, a pose); nothing is as it is made out to be. Thus: 'So', he says, 'the histories say, and it is all quite wrong, as anyone who cares to look into the matter can easily convince himself' (p. 835).

This statement is expanded in the opening of Book IX in a tirade extending to two and a quarter pages, from which it will be sufficient to quote one passage:

'. . . On the 12th of June 1812 the forces of Western Europe crossed the Russian frontier and war began, that is, an event took place opposed to human reason and to human nature. Millions of men perpetrated against one another such innumerable crimes, frauds, treacheries, thefts, forgeries, issues of false money, burglaries, incendiarisms and murders as in whole centuries are not recorded in the annals of all the law-courts of the world, but which those who committed them did not at the time regard as being crimes.

'What produced this extraordinary occurrence? What

were its causes? The historians tell us with naïve assurances etc. . . .' (p. 663).

Nor does Tolstoy's scepticism confine itself to historians. Writing of Natasha's illness he says: 'Doctors came to see her singly and in consultation; talked much in French, German and Latin . . . and prescribed a great variety of medicines for all the diseases known to them, but the simple idea never occurred to any of them that they could not know the disease Natasha was suffering from, as no disease suffered by a live man can be known, for every living person has his own peculiarities and always has his own peculiar, personal, novel, complicated disease unknown to medicine' (p. 721).

One further quotation will not come amiss here. This is a passage dealing with self-assurance. Although only part of this passage is strictly relevant, this part will best be understood in its context:

'A Frenchman is self-assured because he regards himself personally both in mind and body as irresistibly attractive to men and women. An Englishman is self-assured as being a citizen of the best organised state in the world, and therefore, as an Englishman, always knows what he should do and that what he does is undoubtedly correct. An Italian is self-assured because he is excitable and easily forgets himself and other people. *A Russian is self-assured just because he knows nothing and does not want to know anything, since he does not believe that anything can be known.* [My italics.] The German's self-assurance is worst of all, stronger and more repulsive than any other, because he imagines that he knows the truth—science—which he has himself invented but which is for him the absolute truth' (p. 704).

I have spoken of a changed atmosphere in *War and Peace*, dating this change from the opening of Book IX (p. 663). It is not simply that from here on things are treated more soberly, but that whereas hitherto the two sections, the chapters dealing with War and those dealing with Peace possessed an overall, uniform character—we witnessed war through the eyes of persons we knew in a peace-time setting, persons familiar to us, whose fortunes we followed with eager interest and affection—from now on a disunity creeps in. Not only is Tolstoy increasingly forced to have recourse to new characters, who, as in real life it may be argued, make their exits and their entrances, but among whom, nevertheless, we lose sight for whole chapters of those we know, with whom we are involved, so that our interest inevitably flags. Not only do we miss the interaction, the connections between the emotions of a Nicholas Rostov and the actions of Napoleon—we are subjected to abstractions, to summaries, to theories, to diatribes against historians. In Book XIII, for example, comprising ninety-five pages (pp. 1089-1184) we have forty-seven pages in which our most intimate companion is the Commander-in-Chief, Kutuzov.

Not content with continuously flogging this very dead horse (history) throughout the main body of the novel, we find, when we come to the end of the book, not one but two epilogues in which Tolstoy vents his still mounting rage. Let us examine some of the remarks he makes in these epilogues.

I take the first (pp. 1245 ff):

'According to their [the historians'] accounts a reaction took place at that time in Russia also, and the chief culprit was Alexander I, the same man who, according to them, was the chief cause of the liberal movement at the commencement of his reign, as well as of saving Russia. . .

'In what does the substance of their reproaches lie?

'It lies in the fact that an historical figure like Alexander I, standing on the highest possible pinnacle of human power with the blinding light of history focussed upon him—a character exposed to those strongest of all influences, the intrigues, flattery and self-deception inseparable from power—a character who at every moment of his life felt a responsibility for all that was happening in Europe; and not a fictitious but a live character who like every man had his personal habits, passions and impulses towards goodness, beauty and truth—that this character, not lacking in virtue (the historians do not accuse him of that) had not the same conception of the welfare of humanity fifty years ago, as a professor who from his youth upwards, has been occupied with learning—that is, with books and lectures and with taking notes from them.

'But even if we assume that fifty years ago Alexander I was mistaken in his view of what was good for people, we must inevitably assume that the historian who judges Alexander will also, after the lapse of time, turn out to be mistaken in his view of what was good for humanity. This assumption is all the more natural and inevitable because, watching the movement of history, we see that every year, and with each new writer, opinion as to what is good for mankind changes; so that what once seemed good, ten years later seems bad and vice versa. And what is more we find quite contradictory views as to what is good and what is bad in history. Some people regard giving a constitution to Poland or forming the Holy Alliance as praiseworthy in Alexander, while others regarded it as blameworthy.

'The activity of Alexander or of Napoleon cannot be called useful or harmful for it is impossible to say for what it was useful or harmful. . . .'

The second epilogue (pp. 1305-1344) takes different schools of historians and damns them all systematically. It contains such ideas as the following:

(a) that power was held by historians 'to be the collective will of the people, transferred, by expressed or tacit consent, to their chosen rulers. . . .'

(b) '. . . Why then was Napoleon III a criminal when he was taken prisoner at Boulogne, and why, later on, were those criminals whom he arrested?'

(c) 'What causes historical events? Power. What is power? Power is the collective will of the people transferred to one person. Under what conditions is the collective will of the people transferred to one person? On condition that that person expresses the will of the whole people. That is, power is power; in other words power is a word the meaning of which we do not understand.'

We have finished *War and Peace*. We put down the book with the sense that Tolstoy does not notice our departure, so occupied is he wielding his axe, felling the forest around him. We creep away, leaving him still at it, or perhaps we should change the image and say still grappling, a Lear-like figure, wrestling with the problem of free will.

It may appear that I have quoted at disproportionate length. These are mere hints, mere snippets of what is expounded, expanded, insisted upon throughout *War and Peace*. To quote at some length is indispensable if one is to give any idea of Tolstoy's hectoring tone, to establish what as if by some curious conspiratorial reverence is so generally ignored: that this is not the stuff of which literature is made. That if Tolstoy himself later wrote *What is Art* this is not surprising. *War and Peace* is not a work of art written before Tolstoy succumbed to philistinism—the seeds of what came later are all there as they are not there (and this is the paradox, the great mystery) in its successor *Anna Karenina*.

But I will return to this later. My immediate task is to try to sort out as briefly as possible the right from the wrong in *War and Peace*. The fact is the two are inextricably mixed. If *War and Peace* remains for all its dogmatism a great, some claim the greatest of all novels— is this not, in part, due to that which also gives it its weakness, to Tolstoy's passion, his fanaticism?

But let us ourselves look for a moment at what it is that the unhappy historian tries to do. Armed with as many facts as he can muster he attempts to give some account of what took place in the past. His account must, of necessity, to some extent be false since much of what occurred went unrecorded and much was accidental, irrational in character, and not explicable or logical. Life, as lived at the time, is not clear but confused. It is not merely that from his later vantage point the historian is able to see the pattern the living could not see. Different patterns emerge for different people. This is not to say that these patterns are wrong. They are aspects, facets of truth, which is all that we can ever have of Truth.

History and life, then, Tolstoy is saying, are two quite different things. And we have no desire to quarrel with him (though we are beginning to see that this may be difficult to avoid). Tolstoy is not concerned to depict history. He is concerned to depict life, to depict the contradictions, the confusion that exists in every sphere, in the army, in Natasha, in history itself, a confusion perpetuated by historians. It is as if the mere idea, the very possibility of anything being clear or logical throws him into a fit of apoplectic rage. No! No! No! It was not like that. It was just the opposite. And he is off, being, without realising, himself clearer and simpler, more dogmatic than anyone else.

This then is one of several reasons why we failed to think of *War and Peace* as an historical novel. Tolstoy not only sets out to refute the historical viewpoint, to give us things as they happen at the time; but in place of heroes and period settings to give us just that feeling of ordinary humdrum reality that seems to us the prerequisite of our own lives, whereas it cannot possibly belong to the lives of those we admire, of heroes, of the famous, actors, film stars, celebrities, etc. In Tolstoy we are at home just as in our own lives; we feel that it is all quite 'everyday', despite the grandeur of the personages among whom we find ourselves. Thus seated in the carriage beside the Commander-in-Chief Kutuzov on the

eve of Austerlitz, we do not feel overawed despite our
knowledge, our recognition that he is a great man. We
perch beside him familiarly as a child might do. And in
fact what we hear and see in *War and Peace* is very much
what a child in those circles might hear and see. We see
how Kutuzov behaves, we hear his words, we sense the
burden he carries as a child might do. In the same way
when we enter Napoleon's presence, we see what the
child would have seen: a small, plump, dapper man
apparently fresh and relaxed from the bath; we observe
his clothes, his vanity, his spoilt-child's behaviour. If
what we are shown is a sort of white cockatoo; if this
method appears superficial here; if indeed in the case of
Napoleon it is Tolstoy's intention to debunk, to depict
the pettiness, the essential insignificance of this man on
whom the destiny of nations hangs—what the child sees
is not irrelevant. It is Napoleon's insignificance that is
terrifying. And we recall the thoughts of Prince Andrew,
who so often seems to echo what Tolstoy himself says
elsewhere in the text: ' "Not only does a good commander
not need any special qualities, on the contrary he needs
the absence of the highest and best human attributes—
love, poetry, tenderness and philosophic enquiring doubt.
He should be limited." '

I have spoken of the peculiarly youthful joyfulness of
the world we first enter in *War and Peace*, of how at
home we feel in this world, of how in it we recapture
both the vision and the happiness of childhood. And yet
to enter this world is to enter one which has completely
vanished. It is like one of those rambling country houses,

filled with children and dogs, where there are huge log fires, where the grandparents live and the family assembles; where one rides a lot and is healthy and cheerful and exuberant, where the generations meet and mix but can also escape from each other, and take refuge in libraries, fade away into parks and nursery wings. This way of life has gone and with it, perhaps most marked in its absence, the easy exchange between the generations. Children in *War and Peace* do not rebel against their parents. They love and honour and confide in them. The fact that old Prince Bolkonski is a great man, an autocrat and quite unbearable, does not make his son a weakling or, as it would today, inspire resentment in him. Nor does the fact that Prince Andrew in some ways resembles his father make them, as it might, incompatible. Following in his father's footsteps Prince Andrew enters the army; later, to help him, he serves under him.

Today family life is largely felt as claustrophobic. And yet even those who were unhappy children, who were never at home in their own homes, whose home life did not have, as it were, its own private language, its own special unique brand of humdrum homeliness, even such people, I think, will know what I mean, will recognise this homeliness in the pages of *War and Peace*—if only as something they themselves have missed.

The note is struck at the outset, at Anna Sherer's soirée, a first chapter which, on a first reading, people tend to find so confusing that far from feeling at home, they tend to feel utterly at sea. It is impossible, they complain, to grasp who is who, and then there are all those ghastly Russian names, all sounding exactly the same and the women with different endings and added to this diminutives, variations. They must confess they nearly gave up. But 'once you are through this chapter', friends assure them, 'it is all plain sailing'. And from henceforward they will be among those who, for the rest of their lives, continue to re-read *War and Peace*.

The very same thing which originally made them feel at sea is now precisely what makes them feel at home; and this despite the fact that it is some time since they have read it and they cannot quite remember who everyone is; for no one, this is the point, is introduced to us. People are introduced to one another and in this way, but only, as it were, accidentally, we glean a certain amount of information. Princess Lise chatters to us, we wander from group to group, for we too are old friends, *habitués*, even if, like Pierre Bezhukov, we have been away and only recently returned to Moscow.

We are at home and how much at home! For we are not, as I have said, overawed by all these princes and princesses. Why should we be? The grandeur of these people is purely social. They themselves are simple and ordinary. What even, we may ask, the Czars and Kutuzovs and Napoleons? And apart from them, what about Prince Andrew? Well, Prince Andrew, I concede, may be a special case. For the moment I will confine myself to saying that he is the only character, or the only one we know well, who is neither naïve nor corrupt.

Meanwhile, if we do, to an extent, hobnob with the great, if the Czar attends Natasha's first ball, we catch only glimpses of them, as in real life. It is true that we sometimes know what they are thinking, a thing we could not do in real life, but then in life we can no more see into the minds of the humble than the great.

And here we touch on a further possible reason for failing to think of this book as an historical novel. It is not in the class of those books that give us in historical form the life and times of a Louis XIV. It is about family life, about ordinary Russian people, chiefly members of the ruling class but including a cross-section of the whole of Russian society between 1805 and 1812. Just as Platon, the peasant, makes his appearance, so do the great make theirs, and as human beings, not as mere figure-heads, but nor as central characters. We pass the night with Napoleon before Borodino; we hear his words, and no doubt these are his very words taken by Tolstoy from Napoleon's writings—such words as the questions he asks: ' "Do you know, Rapp, what military art is? It is the art of being stronger than the enemy at a given moment. That's all." ' We go further; we are even told (and, no doubt, again by Napoleon himself in his own words) how he felt at the sight of Moscow prostrate at his feet; we overhear him talking to himself, that is to say we observe the attitudes he strikes for his own benefit even when alone. But we still see him from the outside. The thoughts remain as external as the tight-fitting white trousers. This is as close as we come to Napoleon—as close as he comes to himself, in other words as close as one can come, close enough to see, as the child sees, the grandiose gesture, the absurdity.

If we are still, at our closest to him, remote from Napoleon, we are at this moment very close to Tolstoy. There is nothing Tolstoy abominates so much as poses,

self-deception (a Berg, a Prince Vasili), what does not
spring from the heart, insincerity—all largely adult fail-
ings. Conversely the virtue he sets above all else is simplicity. His heroes are not the great but the ordinary,
even for much of the book still children or adolescents.
What he prizes in the adult is the child. This outlook
finds its natural culmination in the central, not un-
Myshkin-like figure of Pierre Bezhukov. Tolstoy himself practises what he preaches. We see him preparing
himself, paring away at this seemingly artless style in his
early books, in *Family Happiness* and in *Childhood,
Boyhood and Youth*, books which he later came to regard
as worthless. It is illuminating to note, *en passant*, the
strangeness of the grounds on which he denounced
Childhood, Boyhood and Youth, on the grounds of its
'insincerity', which he explains by saying that it could
not be otherwise, since what he was depicting was not
his own childhood but an imaginary one compounded
from those of his friends. There is a strange confusion
here between the reality of life and the truth of art, of the
imagination. But, as someone is quick to remind us, this
judgement belongs to a later period, the period of *What
is Art*. He had, in fact, already rejected these works much
earlier—as we always, perhaps, reject our early work,
embarrassed by its gaucheries. But the confusion, I sus-
pect, was there from the start. The style, that deceptively
simple style forged with so much care, is already the style
of a fanatic. It is characteristically Russian; it has much in
common with Chekov, with Lermontov, with Turgenev
and Dostoevsky, with this difference—that it is pregnant
with intolerance, with irritation. The confusion between

17

art and life, art and morality, reflects the dichotomy in Tolstoy, a dichotomy commonly recognised, but which, in my view, shows itself earlier than is generally allowed; is there even when in his picture, his understanding of childhood and youth, his art is at its height; there, no less than in Proust, in his evident nostalgia—if we still doubt it, there in his own words, in the early diary he kept as a young man in the Caucasus: 'All the first impulses of the heart are pure and lofty. Actual life destroys their innocence and charm.'

We ourselves can still return with pleasure to these early works and find in them the authentic Tolstoyan genius: To the cherry-picking scene in *Family Happiness*, written some five years before his marriage, but which is so moving precisely because it so exactly catches the tenuous character of such happiness; so that we ourselves, as we read, find ourselves holding our breath for fear we may be detected and break the spell; a happiness that moves us because it is so transient, already pregnant with disillusionment. In Sergei Milhailovyich, Tolstoy gives us a man clutching at hope, at a happiness which he knows to be a mirage.

Yes, it is all there, including the powers of dissection, the marvellous directness cutting through inessentials; and the preservation of inessentials, the inconsequential character of real-life conversations, talk which is random but in which, to achieve this effect, Tolstoy cannot afford a waste remark; the disarming child's honesty which, anticipating psychiatry, acknowledges the force of the irrational.

WAR AND PEACE

It is an art which we see, brought to its perfection in *War and Peace*, in Nicholas Rostov's visit to Boris, for instance.

Still fresh from and intoxicated by his first experience of battle, we watch Nicholas setting off, proud of his odd clothes, his shabby appearance 'that of a fighting hussar who had been under fire', and which cannot, he is confident, fail to impress his childhood friend Boris, in the guards.

Both Boris and Nicholas feel they have greatly changed and are anxious for the other to see these changes. Nicholas cannot help swaggering and talking somewhat too loudly. Boris has been moving in smart circles; he has not yet seen any fighting but he has marched with the Tsarevitch and everywhere there have been balls, receptions. No doubt there has also been considerable expense. The only son of an impecunious widow, Boris cannot afford to throw his money about. To Nicholas it is natural to run up debts. Nicholas calls for wine. Boris reluctantly orders some. Meanwhile Nicholas opens a letter from home, sent to him care of Boris and enclosing, together with a sum of money, a letter of recommendation. This letter obtained by his mother, fearful for her son, will procure him a job on the staff of Prince Bagration. Nicholas does not scruple to voice his contempt for adjutants; he will not be anyone's lackey. Boris's reply that one must think of one's career leads Nicholas to look at him 'searchingly'.

Thus meeting far from home, these two, friends from childhood, succeed only in misunderstanding one another. Everything makes for disaster, including the presence and anecdotes of the, as always, complacent Berg. Nicholas has his arm in a sling. Boris tactfully asks how he got his wound. Nicholas, who was a truthful young man and would on no account have told a lie, tells them 'of how . . . he had flown like a storm at the square, cut his way in, slashed to right and left, how his sabre had tasted flesh and he had fallen exhausted . . .' since 'he could not tell them simply that everyone went at a trot and that he fell off his horse and sprained his arm and then ran as fast as he could from a Frenchman into a wood' (p. 258).

In the midst of this thrilling description, Prince Andrew enters the room. His composure puts the cadet off his stride, bringing to a crux all the mixed, pent-up emotions arising from the sense of his false position—anger with all these dandified guardsmen, the feeling that he has not received the accolade he should have had, but has himself, in fact, behaved badly, but that this is not his fault. He at once adopts an insulting tone to Prince Andrew, implies that he too is a lackey and manages within minutes to bring things to the verge of a duel.

Prince Andrew behaves perfectly, as even Nicholas angrily riding home, thinking of all the things he might have said if he had only thought of them in time, and wondering what to do about the duel, is forced to admit: How he would have liked to see 'the fright of that small, frail but proud man when covered by his pistol, and then he felt with surprise that of all the men he knew there was none he would so much like to have for a friend' (p. 260).

No passage, perhaps, in literature more powerfully evokes one's youth, more graphically charts its erratic

course, the degree to which one's behaviour was dictated
by that of others, the small things which could knock one
off one's balance, the unsureness which might then unseat
one altogether, the unnerving experience, peculiar to
youth, of finding oneself behaving as strangely as a
stranger, the rapidity of the transition from hate to
love.

Nicholas Rostov is not a particularly interesting character. He grows up to be a typical country-squire, limited,
somewhat coarse-grained. We begin to lose interest in
him, and the affair with Princess Mary seems contrived.
We wonder at the time of the courtship what she sees in
him; she seems so much the stronger character. In fact
she finds in Nicholas exactly what she sees; just as she
turns out not to be the bigot we took her for, but appears
before us transformed and softened by marriage. The
relationship of this husband and wife might well strike
people today as extraordinary, if not actually sickening.
Violence and not timidity are the climate, the tone in
which contemporary couples conduct their differences.
Unexpectedly this marriage and its success are wholly
convincing; unexpectedly, too, Nicholas earns our respect. We understand, as his rich wife does not, his
preoccupation with crops, his need, as it were, to square
the account, to atone for his father's improvidence. And
we sympathise with Tolstoy's love for him, his rejection
in Nicholas of the desire to improve the peasants' lot, his
insistence that the estate must be made to pay, that this
will be best for everyone including the peasants themselves. Liberalism is all new-fangled nonsense. Nicholas

is the plain man. He is said to be modelled on Tolstoy's own father. There is little doubt who as a human being is worth more in Tolstoy's eyes, which of the two interests him the more or how he prefers to pass his time, with the Emperor Napoleon or hunting with Nicholas and his wolfhound Milka.

Ultimately only in Nicholas, or so it seems to me, does what Tolstoy is trying to say come off.

'But Natasha,' I hear voices on all sides beginning to clamour, 'What about Natasha? Where is she? Surely she is the one who matters? Why do you speak of that boring Nicholas, that stick Princess Mary when it is she, Natasha, whom Tolstoy loves, who for him enshrines all the virtues?—Natasha the incarnation of youth, artlessness, spontaneity, who is herself both the embodiment and the culmination of all that Tolstoy strove for in his art. Only a child could understand Natasha.'

I am not so sure I agree. I am not at all sure, that is, that Tolstoy is as successful with Natasha as with Nicholas. But surely, the reader objects, if only as a portrait of a child the thing is unsurpassed? Well, yes, as a child I concede Natasha to be charming. And later she is still brilliantly observed—her behaviour to Anna Dimitrievna after the Anatole Kuràgin débâcle for instance, could not be better done. But she is not, it seems to me, known, felt from inside to the same extent that Nicholas is. Perhaps this is simply because we do in fact see a great deal of her from the outside, through the eyes of other people. Through the eyes of the Countess who exclaims: ' "Dear, dear! Just look at her!" ' pointing to

Natasha, who, 'assuming quite the pose of a society woman', was 'fanning herself and smiling over the fan, (p. 71); through the eyes of the Count and of his servant Simon who admire her riding; of 'Uncle' for whom she dances to the balalaika; of Nicholas in the troyka thinking: 'How charming this Natasha of mine is. I have no other friend like her, and never shall have. Why should she marry? We might always drive about together' (p. 560); through the eyes, even, of Helène, who at the height of her beauty, and in the midst of a crowded opera house is made by Tolstoy to glance 'attentively' at Natasha.

We see her through the eyes of her lovers, Pierre and Prince Andrew. But everyone in the book loves Natasha and we too are invited to love, to fall in love with her as we are not invited to do with Nicholas. Sonia and Princess Mary may be in love with him but we are not caught up into their feelings, we do not find him romantic; we do not lose our hearts to the hero Pierre. He is patently unromantic; but nor are we in danger of falling for the more heroic Andrew. Even when we are shown Natasha from the inside we are still, we may feel, seeing her as Pierre sees her. (The scene in which half ironically she looks at herself in the glass and thinks: How charming she is that Natasha, pretty, intelligent, graceful, and her voice is excellent, and, yes, she dances too quite divinely— an episode not in itself unlikely or unconvincing, but in which it seems as if Tolstoy were expressing, were unconsciously giving expression to our sense that even when Natasha is alone we are looking on.)

The fact is we cannot without discomfort, without self-praise that is, feel ourselves in Natasha's shoes, as we do in those of Nicholas visiting Boris, for instance. It is not that Tolstoy does not understand women. No one, no woman writer even, has understood them better, as is established by *Anna Karenina*, by his action in writing a book on this subject and by his portrayal of types as different as Anna herself and Dolly. But Natasha is not a woman; she is never allowed to become one. In contrast to the voluptuous Hélène, whose appearance at eighteen suggests a woman of thirty, Natasha is maintained in a state of childhood, with her arms hanging down at her sides as she sings or waits to be asked to dance. Natasha, in fact, never leaves the nursery—she is conveyed safely straight from childhood to motherhood, leaving out the bedroom in between.

'All the first impulses of the heart are pure and lofty. Actual life destroys their innocence and charm.' It certainly effectually destroys Natasha's charm. But at first for a moment we are incredulous. Can this stout blowzy woman, wearing some loose garment, apparently convenient for breast-feeding, really be that Natasha, that girl who ran past Prince Andrew in the garden, whose existence, whose voice on the balcony, sufficed to awake in him 'an unreasoning springtime feeling of joy and renewal?'

We flick back the pages and tot up the dates. The book starts in 1805. In 1805 Natasha was thirteen. At twenty-one, when she marries Pierre, she is still charming. In 1820 she is twenty-eight. But she looks at least forty. 'Natasha', we read, 'did not follow the golden rule, advocated by clever folk, especially the French, which says that a girl should not let herself go when she

marries. . . . Natasha, on the contrary, had at once abandoned all her witchery, of which her singing had been an
unusually powerful part. She gave it up just because it
was so powerfully seductive. She took no pains with her
manners . . . or with her toilet . . . or to avoid incon-
veniencing her husband by being too exacting' (p. 1274).
She is, in fact, nothing if not exigent. Not only is the way
she has let herself go '. . . a habitual subject of jest to
those about her', but so too is her jealousy: 'She was
jealous of Sonya, of the governess, of every woman
pretty or plain. Pierre not only dared not flirt with, but
dared not even speak smilingly to any other woman; did
not dare to dine at the club as a pastime, did not dare to
spend money on a whim. The general opinion was that
Pierre was under his wife's thumb, which was really true'
(p. 1276).

We feel as one may feel on returning to a place—to
Paris, to some *quartier* we have known, sacred to us by
reason of its associations, the names of the poets and
artists who have lived there, the colours of the shop
fronts, its unique local flavour, its walled gardens—to
find it pulled down, its streets erased, its quality gone for
ever, replaced by blocks of concrete offices.

For Natasha too has gone for ever; she too has been
erased. She who possessed the power to re-awaken in
men like Pierre and Prince Andrew new hope, feelings
they had thought dead, to bring them back to a sense of
the beauty of life, of its joy and fullness, to feel this as one
may hear the sound of water running again in brooks that
have been frozen, or as those who have lost their hearing may feel on regaining it, and once more hearing

Beethoven or Mozart—this Natasha is lost to us. In place of her we now have a Natasha, the reverse of her former self, a creature wholly occupied with mundane considerations in whom life is reduced to its most basic function, the reproduction of beings who will reproduce themselves, a woman still young, who, the wife of a rich man, can think of nothing better than kopecks and babies' napkins, whose behaviour is devoid of grace or charm, whose existence is a denial of life, contracted to a point where it no longer seems to us worth living.

We are utterly at a loss. We recognise Princess Mary; Nicholas is a coherent character; Pierre is unchanged. But this later Natasha seems to us a wholly arbitrary choice on Tolstoy's part. She might equally well, it seems to us, have turned out quite differently, have filled any one of a dozen different roles. For Natasha, yes, we realise it now (this was her charm), was capable, as Princess Mary was not, of transformation. Her's was the rainbow, chameleon receptivity of youth. Most women are formed by their husbands. And particularly one would have thought, would this be so with Natasha, the wife of a man so much older than herself. If Pierre was in some ways weak he would have been strengthened by marriage. What might not have been made of a Natasha with her quickness, her sensitivity, her capacity for pleasure, her high spirits subdued by her long sadness, a Natasha in love . . .?

But our speculations, our musings are cut short. It dawns on us that Tolstoy is not deploring but actually recommending what seems to us so monstrous. If, for the first few horrified moments we took him to be ironic, to be giving us a dose of reality, to be saying grimly 'This, you

see, is what happens to your Natashas', we quickly recognise that we are wrong. The tone is not ironic but para-
doxical. It is clear that he intends to shock; that he is at
his most difficult, in his most perverse mood. Not only
does he anticipate our reaction. He is bent on provoking
it. The antipathy he feels for us at this moment is, we
perceive with amusement, quite equal to the antipathy he
feels for historians.

Well, we, at least, can smugly decline to descend to his
level. We are sweetly determined to be reasonable. Our
impressions, moreover, of what we have read are, we
must admit, confused; we feel as if we had been hit on
the head with a truncheon. No doubt we have misunderstood. We had better go back. And back we totter,
still suffering from shock, still secretly hoping, believing
that it will all be different, that we cannot really have
seen what we thought we saw—Natasha come striding
dishevelled from the nursery in her dressing-gown and
with joyful face 'show us a yellow instead of a green
stain on baby's napkin' (p. 1276).

Dutifully then we turn back and force ourselves to
swallow the description of the figure 'stouter and broader'
of this 'handsome fertile woman', in whom it is hard 'to
recognise the slim lively Natasha of former days'. We
struggle on. But no—it really is too much—here she is at
it again with the napkin. We put the book aside and this
time we do not muse. Staring blankly before us we ask—
'Why?'

The answer, the clue to the early as well as the later
Natasha is to be found where we least think of looking

for it, in the declaration that sexual love 'is something abominable, swinish, which it is horrid and shameful to remember'; that 'it is not for nothing that nature has made it disgusting and shameful'. These words occur in the *Kreutzer Sonata*, a short book written some twenty years after *War and Peace*.

But I will perhaps make myself clearer if I append one further passage describing the change in Natasha on her marriage.

'To fluff out her curls, put on fashionable dresses, and sing romantic songs to fascinate her husband would have seemed as strange as to adorn herself to attract herself. To adorn herself for others might perhaps have been agreeable—she did not know—but she had no time at all for it. The chief reason for devoting no time either to singing, to dress, or to choosing her words, was that she really had not time to spare for those things' (pp. 1274-1275).

It is with something of a shock, the shock of recognition, that we come on this passage in the *Kreutzer Sonata*.

' "You see it is only we men who don't know . . . what women know very well, that the most exalted poetic love depends not on moral qualities, but on physical nearness, and on the coiffeur, and on the colour and cut of the dress. Ask an expert coquette who has set herself the task of captivating a man, which she would prefer to risk: to be convicted in his presence of lying, of cruelty, or even dissoluteness, or to appear before him in an ugly or badly made dress—she will always prefer the first. . . .

' "A woman . . . knows very well that *all the talk about*

elevated subjects [my italics] is just talk, but that what a man wants is her body and all that presents it in the most deceptive but alluring light. . . . You say that the women of our society have other interests in life than prostitutes have, but I say no, and will prove it. If people differ in the aims of their lives, by the inner content of their lives, this difference will necessarily be reflected in externals and their externals will be different. But look at those unfortunate despised women and at the highest society ladies: the same costumes, the same fashions, the same perfumes, the same exposure of arms, shoulders and breasts, the same tight skirts over prominent bustles, the same passion for stones, for costly glittering objects, the same amusements, dances, music and singing. As the former employ all means to allure, so do these others." '

We no longer ask why Natasha has 'abandoned all her witchery'. It would place her on a par with a prostitute.

The clue to the child, the girl Natasha, as well as to Pierre's wife, lies, I have said, where we least expect to find it, in the violence of Tolstoy's sexual drives and in the no less violent disgust these aroused in him, a disgust which comes to extend not merely to his own behaviour but to sex itself:

' "Love? Love is an exclusive preference for one person over everybody else" said the lady.

' "Preference for how long? A month, two days, or half an hour?", said the grey-haired man and began to laugh.'

' "Every man", ' he insisted, ' "experiences what you call love for every pretty woman." '

The fact that after his marriage, he could desire other

women, that desire could exist unaccompanied by love, never ceased to revolt Tolstoy.

' "It is not merely this impossibility, [of exclusive love] but the inevitable satiety. To love one person for a whole lifetime is like saying that one candle will burn a whole life." '

This statement is qualified. It is not that constancy is, in itself, impossible, but that it is made so by debauchery, by the promiscuity regarded as natural for men before marriage.

Thus ' "I began," ' said the grey-haired man, ' "to indulge in debauchery as I began to drink and smoke. . . . I had become what is called a libertine. To be a libertine is a physical condition, like that of a morphinist, a drunkard or a smoker. As a morphinist, a drunkard, or a smoker is no longer normal, so too a man who has known several women for his pleasure is no longer normal, but is a man perverted for ever, a libertine." '

He described his marriage, the honeymoon, and here there occurs one of Tolstoy's most appalling statements:

' "Pleasure from smoking, just as from that, if it comes at all, comes later. The husband must cultivate that vice in his wife in order to derive pleasure from it." '

The violence of his sexual urges made Tolstoy fanatical. It is their force that creates the puritan. Not only must men, no less than women, be virgins when they marry, even when married they may not sleep with their wives when they are pregnant or breast-feeding (and his insistence that mothers must breast-feed their children, and not employ wet-nurses, as was the custom in Russia, comes itself to seem like flagellation).

But to return briefly to the text of the *Kreutzer Sonata* at the point where we abandoned it:

' "Why vice?" I said, "you are speaking of the most natural human functions."

' "Natural?" he said, "Natural? No, I may tell you that I have come to the conclusion that it is, on the contrary, *un*natural. Yes, quite *un*natural. Ask a child, ask an unperverted girl. . . . It is natural to eat, and to eat is, from the very beginning, enjoyable, easy, pleasant and not shameful; but this is horrid, shameful and painful. . . . And an unspoilt girl, as I have convinced myself, always hates it." '

It is common practice to regard *War and Peace* as literature and the *Kreutzer Sonata* as a tract. The latter, however, still shocks us. What must its impact have been when it was written? Today it is the tone, less than the matter which shocks, the violence, the unbalance, the desperation.

' "But permit me," ' says the lawyer in the *Kreutzer Sonata*, ' "Facts contradict you . . . many people honourably live long married lives. . . ." '

The grey-haired man again laughs. Husbands and wives merely deceive people. They pretend to be monogamists while living polygamously. ' "That is bad, but still bearable. But when, as most frequently happens, the husband and wife have undertaken the external duty of living together all their lives and begin to hate each other after a month, and wish to part but still continue to live together, it leads to that terrible hell which makes people take to drink, shoot themselves and kill or poison themselves or one another. . . ." '

This is a far cry—could one imagine anything further from the tone of *War and Peace*? No wonder the two works are placed in different categories: on the one hand a crackpot sociological outburst—the hysteria, if you like, of a man who has admittedly suffered much in his own domestic life—and on the other the Rostov household. The two things are poles apart.

To my mind they are inseparably connected.

But turning away from Natasha herself, let us look for a moment more closely at her parents, the old Rostovs.

For the first thing that strikes us about them is their antiquity. Countess Rostova married at sixteen. At the start of the book her oldest child Vera is seventeen. Thus the Countess could be thirty-four. Tolstoy makes her older. She is forty-five and worn out with child-bearing; she has borne the Count twelve children of whom four survive. Somehow this fact fails to register, partly perhaps because we are told it too early and too baldly—it comes in our introduction to the Countess, in whom, since we do not yet know her, we feel little interest. But also because our interest is never aroused. For some reason what we are told does not make us sympathetic. It makes us feel that the Countess is a bore.

And it may seem to us that we were right. After some thirteen hundred-odd pages we may feel that we know her little better. And this feeling is doubtless confirmed by our final view of her, irritably playing patience with her companion; by the fact 'that she ate, drank, slept and kept awake but did not live', that 'life gave her no new impressions'. We show her little mercy. If old people are bored or boring they have only themselves to blame. Our harshness may even prompt us to reflect that Tolstoy himself is somewhat harsh in his summary treatment of her. The point, surely, is not that she has *had* twelve children but that out of twelve, eight have died; that the Countess has lived in constant torment. At the time when we come on the scene moreover, Petya is only nine. The Countess's terror when anyone fell ill, the sad time this family has lived through is still recent history. How is it that we find no trace of it ? That the shadow which must have darkened the early lives of Nicholas and Natasha is, quite literally, never mentioned?

But wait, no, there is one reference. How was it we overlooked it? It occurs some eight pages on (p. 43).

' "How plainly all these young people wear their hearts on their sleeves", said Anna Mikhaylovna, pointing to Nicholas as he went out. "*Cousinage—dangereux voisinage*" ' she added.

' "Yes", said the Countess when the brightness these young people had brought into the room had vanished; and as if answering a question which no one had put to her, but which was always on her mind, "and how much suffering, how much anxiety one has had to go through that one might rejoice in them now. And yet really the anxiety is greater now than the joy. One is always, always anxious! Especially just at this age, so dangerous both for girls and boys." '

But even here, in this passage, the reference is oblique. The Countess is not so much bemoaning past sorrows, as complaining that things get worse and not better as time goes on. It does not so much remind us of what she has gone through, as have the effect of minimising, making light of this. We do not so much recall as forget her sufferings, which she now replaces with ordinary anxiety, anxiety as common to parents as it is useless. Fresh from our first encounter with the Rostov family, dazzled, intrigued as if in an aviary by our glimpses of all these gay, darting, youthful figures, intoxicated by the air we breathe, that sunlit, buoyant, crystalline air peculiar to the household, the Countess's *douleurs* seem oddly mal à propos.

Tolstoy tells us that she is 'languid' and that this gives her an 'air of distinction'. But if the rate of infant mortality was high, if the Countess's plight is common, this does not make it less painful, less strange that when she confides in an old friend: ' "Ah, my dear, my life is not all roses either . . ." ' what she is referring to is money.

It is true that the old Count is feckless and that this comes home to roost. But even the fact that the Rostovs lose their money is, one feels, itself a commendation in Tolstoy's eyes, part and parcel of their unworldliness, of the old Count's lack of self-interest, of his trusting childlike nature, the penalty rather of virtue than of vice; the penalty of living life as it should be lived, as it is lived in that charming Rostov household, in that simple, lively, unpretentious childhood paradise. . . . And despite the fact that we get to know them in Moscow we do, in fact, if we think of the Rostovs, tend to picture a garden, an unspoilt, overgrown garden in early June, a garden of tangled paths, high with cow-parsley, adazzle with apple-blossom and gay with birds—with children's voices that echo and die, muffled, extinguished like tapers in the tomb-like salons and ante-chambers of the world where old Count Bezhukov lies dying, where Prince Vasili waits, where ambition and corruption dwell.

But how old is Prince Vasili? He is 'near sixty'. But once again this fact makes no impression. Elegant, urbane, the Prince is the typical courtier; as far as we are concerned he is ageless. His children are all grown up. They are older than the Rostovs. And yet the Prince is never 'The old Prince'—whereas Count Rostov is seldom referred to except as 'The old Count'.

But then the Prince would never 'waddle in' to his wife's bedroom with the *sauté de madère* he has been tasting spilt down the front of his evening waistcoat (and which the Countess proceeds to scrub off with her cambric handkerchief).

To suggest that the appellation is one used in the household to distinguish Count Rostov from his sons, as English servants might speak of 'The Master' will not do (Prince Vasili has himself two sons). In this case Count Rostov would be known simply as 'The Count' and his sons as the young Counts, Count Nicholas and Count Petya.

But how old exactly is the Count, fifty-nine or sixty? On the occasion when he dances the Daniel Cooper, he is expressly referred to as 'the amiable old gentleman'. This description seems odd for fifty-nine. And he may, of course, be older. But although the performance clearly is an occasion, although everyone stands around to watch and admire the Count's agility, no one seems to think he will have a stroke.

The fact is, if we think about it, that old people are older in the Rostov household than outside it. There they are background figures. Their lives are already over. It is the children whom we, the reader, come to see. This does not strike us as odd as it must do in life were we to visit the houses of people we know not for the sake of the parents, our contemporaries, but for the sake of the children in the school room. The presence of children does not place their parents on the retired list. But let us return to Countess Rostova's drawing-room and listen again, and this time for a little while longer, to the conversation taking place there: ' "One is always, *always* anxious", says the Countess. "Especially at this age, so dangerous, both for girls and boys."

' "It all depends on the bringing up", remarked the visitor.

' "Yes, you're quite right," continued the Countess. "Till now I have always, thank God, been my children's friend and had their full confidence," said she, repeating the mistake of so many parents who imagine that their children have no secrets from them: "I know I shall always be my daughter's first confidante, and that if Nicholas with his impulsive nature does get into mischief (a boy can't help it) he will all the same never be like all those Peterbourg young men."

' "Yes, they are splendid, splendid youngsters," chimed in the Count, who always solved questions that seemed to him perplexing by deciding that everything was splendid. "Just fancy: wants to be a hussar. What's one to do, my dear?"

' "What a charming creature your younger girl is," said the visitor, "a little volcano!"

' "Yes, a regular volcano," said the Count, "Takes after

36

me. And what a voice she has, though she's my daughter
I tell the truth when I say she'll be a second Salomoni" '
(p. 43).

It is easy to open *War and Peace* and come upon some
passage which one has no recollection of ever reading,
partly as, in this case, because our interest has flagged,
because the young people have left the room, because our
interest has followed them out, and partly because what
the old people say is so boring, is so exactly what they
would say, so that one wonders, really, why they bother
to say it. We feel we can take it as read, that we have
nothing to learn from it. We do not pause to reflect that
our reaction, our boredom even, is itself a tribute to
Tolstoy's art, to the lifelike effect he achieves.

The truth is we have entirely forgotten that we are
reading. We respond to these people as we would in life.
Nor do we reflect that we are ourselves no longer children.
For what we have here is again the child's view, not merely
that child's unaffectedness and honesty that Tolstoy strove
for in himself and in his style, but the child's view of
adults as boring. This is a new note. We are not asked
to take these people seriously, to treat their problems as
on a par with those of a Pierre or Natasha. The Countess's
anxiety is stereotyped. If, indeed, Tolstoy struck us as
somewhat harsh in his summary treatment of Countess
Rostova, may it not be that there is an element of the
child's dispassionate cruelty in his attitude? Or is it merely
that it is safer, as children themselves find it safer, to
dispose of adults in this way?

The answer, as I have said, lies in the *Kreutzer Sonata*.
In Tolstoy the cult of the child's view of life, his open

preference for children, implies, it must be faced, a rejection of the adult world.

What is the main distinction between adults and children? The dividing line is puberty, the fundamental distinction the procreative function. We cannot but feel the antiquity of the parents as central to Tolstoy's idyll, to the happiness he depicts in the Rostov household. Why do the Count and Countess not 'hate each other'? Why do they not inhabit that terrible hell which makes people take to drink, shoot themselves and kill or poison themselves or one another'? Because we are kept at a distance, because they are background figures, because we are not allowed to come too close, to see too much, are not invited to take them seriously. Because the Count is always 'The old Count', i.e., because the parents resemble grandparents— they are safely out of the sphere of sexual relations.

War and Peace is a long book. Required from the outset to take on so large a cast of characters, continually called upon to drop one and take up another, we unconsciously tend to make our own selection, to pick out and concentrate on those who interest us most. In our eagerness, moreover, we read too fast. To go back and trace the course of any one character in the book is instructive and may even be disturbing. It may also be pleasurable. Having apparently swallowed entire passages whole, we may now have the additional, if undeserved, enjoyment of discovering a second *War and Peace*.

It is especially rewarding to do this with the luckless Countess, whom, for the obvious reason that she bored us, or interested us so much less than the other characters, supplies us with what is almost a new book, with so much fresh Tolstoy. The Countess herself goes up in our estimation.

Formerly we concurred in Prince Andrew's harsh opinion. Granted the paradox of parents and children, the fact that children cannot be accounted for by their parents, we could not help asking what the Rostovs had done, not to deserve such children, but to deserve their relation with them. How is it that Nicholas, the young hussar, at the age of the greatest idealism and intolerance continues to respect and love the Count? How could Natasha confide in and lean on the weak, *passé* Countess? For Tolstoy expressly tells us that she is weak, that rising from her prayers and seeing Natasha installed in her bed 'she smiled in her kind weak way'. But just as on the occasion of Denisov's proposal her tart reaction is exactly right (she does, if anything, seem rather unduly severe on poor Denisov), so in Natasha's bedtime talk with her mother— if the Countess's side of the tête-à-tête is outweighed in our memory by her daughter's side, we cannot fail to admire the Countess's contribution, her sound good sense, for that is all it is, sympathetic good sense, as Natasha clearly feels. There is, quite simply, no call for severity. The Countess listens and giggles, as Natasha says, like a girl. But she is not like modern parents afraid of their children. She does not scruple to speak her mind.

They are talking of Boris:

' " . . . You know you can't marry him", says the Countess.

' "Why not?" said Natasha, without changing her position.

' "Because he is young, because he is poor, because he is a relation . . . and because you yourself don't love him."

' "How do you know?"

' "I do know. It's not right, darling!"

' "But if I want to . . ." said Natasha.

' "Leave off talking nonsense," said the Countess.

' "But if I want to . . ."

' "Natasha I am in earnest."

' . . . Next day the Countess called Boris aside and had a talk with him after which he ceased coming to the Rostovs.'

The Count and Countess are pictured by Tolstoy as easy-going. But this is very different from being weak. It may indeed express a strength, whereas weakness may take the form of undue severity. Even the Count, in many ways weak, is not being weak with Nicholas when the latter confesses his debt to Dolokhov. He simply loves his son and divines the shame that Nicholas is concealing behind his callousness. His father's failure to be angry with him is, in fact, far more effective than any anger could have been.

To say that the Rostovs' strength is love must appear simpliste. But certainly the demonstrative affection in *War and Peace* between parents and children would be unusual today. But then today such love is too often felt by children as an encumbrance, and parents who indulged it would feel guilty. In the Countess, even, it is not quite normal. An adoring mother to her children she throws no crumb of attention or love to her orphaned niece Sonya, who lives in the house and is brought up with Natasha. Later, she is in fact, extraordinarily brutal to her. But even before the Rostovs lose their money, she has never wanted Sonya to marry Nicholas who loves her. This can only be explained by jealousy. Her own marriage is depicted as a happy one. Nevertheless the Count is inadequate. As a man he has failed her, and she has compensated for this in her feeling for her sons. Thus returning home for dinner Petya tells them the news he has heard, that the order had certainly already been given for everyone to go armed to the Three Hills tomorrow and that there would be a big battle there.

The Countess looked with timid horror at her son's eager, excited face as he said this. She knew that if she said a word about his not going to this battle (she knew he enjoyed the thought of the impending engagement) he would say something about men, honour and the fatherland—something senseless, masculine, obstinate . . . and her plans would be spoilt and so . . . hoping to arrange to leave before this and take Petya with her as their protector, she did not answer him, but after dinner took the Count aside and implored him to take her away quickly, that very night if possible. With a woman's involuntary loving cunning she, who till then had not shown any alarm, said that 'she would die of fright if they did not leave that very night' (p. 945).

The Countess's attitude to men has not, as it might have done, made her a bossy, dominating woman. Had it done so the atmosphere at the Rostovs must have been very different. The resentment, none the less, if suppressed, is there. It makes its appearance briefly but unmistakably, like a snake's tongue, in the chapter 'The Rostovs leave Moscow'.

A DARING COIFFEUR

On hearing that the carts which had been loaded with furniture were now being unloaded to take the wounded, the Countess sends for her husband. He comes to her room and explains: 'The Count spoke timidly as he always did when talking of money matters. The Countess was accustomed to this tone as a precursor of news of something detrimental to the children's interests, such as the building of a new gallery or conservatory, the inauguration of a private theatre or an orchestra. She was accustomed to oppose anything announced in that tone and considered it her duty to do so.

'She assumed her dolefully submissive manner and said to her husband:

' "Listen to me, Count, you have managed matters so that we are getting nothing for the house and now you wish to throw away all our—all the *children's* property! You said yourself that we have a hundred thousand roubles worth of things in the house. . . . It's the government's business to look after the wounded; they know that. Look at the Lopukhins opposite, they cleared out everything two days ago. That's what other people do. It's only we who are such fools. If you have no pity on me, have some for the children."

'Flourishing his arms in despair the Count left the room without replying.

' "Papa, what are you doing that for"? asked Natasha, who had followed him into her mother's room.

' "Nothing! What business is it of yours?" muttered

If you look it is all there—in diminuendo; rather as in one of those Florentine paintings, in which, behind the

Madonna and Child or the saint being martyred, you glimpse a miniature fourteenth-century town, with ordinary life going on, all greatly reduced in scale, diminutive figures emerging from toy houses; a boy is leading a horse away, figures are talking in groups or rather, on closer inspection, it turns out, fighting.

Yes, if you look it is all there, even down to the hatred, the resentment the Countess nurses towards her husband; with this difference that here it is stated with balance, these things are kept in proportion. The very title calls to mind this balance: *War and Peace*; we may visualise the two things weighed in the scales, offset, that is, one against the other. And certainly Tolstoy poses the question; the two sets of conditions are weighed, compared. Which is to be preferred? At least in the first half of *War and Peace* there is little doubt of the answer; War, the happiness of action, the comradeship to be found among men, Nicholas's relief on rejoining his regiment, the relief of a men's world, life without women.

War or Peace? The question must surely strike us as odd. Is this question and this answer the reason for war? The implied human predicament is a terrible one, more terrible still in a newly married man. We picture Tolstoy shut in his study after some marital quarrel and with horror catching himself nostalgically recalling his former military life, its peace of mind, its clear conscience, its straightforwardness, its mutual respect and self-respect, contrasting this with his married state, the pettiness of women, the perpetual misunderstandings, the degradation.

There are persons who, with good reason, find such

pictures in questionable taste. They object to this dragging in of the artist's life. The life may itself be of interest but the two spheres must be kept separate. A poem is either a thing complete in itself, or it is nothing. Thus our dislike of Rilke, the man, should not colour our judgement of the poems.

In this particular case, moreover, the picture is untrue. *War and Peace* was not conceived in this way. It began life under the title *The Year 1805*. As 1805 extended to 1812 Tolstoy actually thought of calling it *All's Well that Ends Well*. Not till December 1867 did an advertisement appear announcing the first three volumes of *War and Peace* by Count Leo Tolstoy, the final title being quite simply appropriated from Proudhon's tract *La Guerre et la Paix*.

It was in fact Sonya, his wife, who, acting as a buffer and relieving him of all material cares, as well as serving as copyist, gave Tolstoy the conditions he needed in which to write *War and Peace*. Later it was this period that she herself mourned, the period in which, deciphering Tolstoy's writing and discussing the book with him, she pathetically looked back to as the time when they were closest and happiest.

It is Sonya whom Tolstoy depicts when he writes: 'At home Natasha placed herself in the position of a slave to her husband and everyone in the household went on tiptoe when he was occupied, that is, was reading and writing in his study.'

This may appear as a lesson to critics to curb their imagination. It does not invalidate my hypothesis. If Tolstoy and his wife declared themselves happy, if the

real unhappiness came later, if their difficulties to begin
with were merely those inherent in the transition from
romance to marriage—it has still to be remembered that
with Tolstoy nothing was life size, was as it was for other
people. His senses, his sensibility, his sufferings, all were
greater. The same, as we have remarked, may be said both
of his sexual drives and the disgust these aroused in him.
Shame perversely made him a brutal lover and Sonya an
unresponsive one. This coupled with Sonya's knowledge
of his past, his pleasure with peasant mistresses, the fact
that she was pregnant which, she felt, made her unattractive to him (thus inspiring in her that jealousy which is to
strike us so strangely, as so unaccountable in Natasha)
transformed the high-spirited girl into a clinging hysteri-
cal wife. Tolstoy, with all his understanding of women,
could only attribute Sonya's behaviour to her pregnancy
and wait in the hope that the birth of the child would both
bring back the old Sonya and leave him free to write. In
fact it was he who caused still further scenes, insisting
that Sonya feed the child despite having cracked nipples;
thus eliciting a letter from Sonya's father, a doctor, in
which he says, 'I see you have both lost your wits'.

Nevertheless Tolstoy's hopes bore fruit. He began to
write again. With Tolstoy safe in his study, Sonya's fears
of his peasant loves abated. Tolstoy too was happier. He
had no time now for brooding on his marriage. With
War and Peace on his hands he could no longer complain
of being occupied by trivialities.

Tolstoy was twenty-nine when he wrote *Family Happiness*, thirty-four when he married Sonya Behrs. A year

later he was already at work on *War and Peace*, the first parts being published in 1867, the remainder by 1869. That the book was begun so soon after his marriage and written during these years is a factor which cannot, I think, be ignored. It accounts both for the difference and the rather frightening resemblance between it and *Family Happiness*.

The sadness always so close to the surface in the earlier book, which partly gives it its lyrical quality, suggesting less a foreknowledge than an outlook already developed which could hardly fail to be destructive, this elegiac note is itself absent from *War and Peace*. Marriage at first brought Tolstoy fresh hope. Later he said that his happiness lasted for six months only. None the less at the time hope remained. Opening *War and Peace* we are less struck than infected by the overflowing light-heartedness, the irrepressible joy in life which will not be contained, which breaking out at the most unlikely moments transfigures, as I have said, even the horrors of battle. This, the irrational joy of youth, of health, comes back to us as something we had ourselves forgotten. The first part of *War and Peace* is frankly nostalgic. The atmosphere of the Rostovs is that of the Behrs family; Tolstoy is depicting the charm of courtship, of his wife before their marriage. The second section is altogether grimmer. In it we see Tolstoy turning his back on the past, struggling to come to terms with reality. The tone is that of a man cornered, goaded, desperate. Historians and generals are not the only ones on whom he vents his impotent rage. Nearer to hand is the medical profession, are the doctors who attend Natasha in her illness. Tolstoy's hatred of doctors is only explained, like so much else in *War and*

Peace, by the *Kreutzer Sonata* in which he speaks of children falling ill, of the mother's panic fed by faith or lack of faith in doctors. Thus speaking of the wife in the *Kreutzer Sonata* he writes:

' "When a child is ill one must get hold of the very best one, the one who saves, and then the child is saved; but if you don't get that doctor, or if you don't live in the place where that doctor lives, the child is lost. This was not a creed peculiar to her, it is the creed of all the women of our class and she heard nothing else from all sides." '

It is impossible not to feel that Tolstoy's intense irritation is here partly directed against his wife. His struggle to come to terms with things as they are reaches its climax in the late Natasha—a picture which reminds one of nothing so much as a man who forces himself to eat what he does not like.

In the case of Tolstoy it not only seems to me justified but essential to take the man as a whole, essential, that is, to a further understanding of *War and Peace*. Almost every character in it has a prototype in life, if not in Tolstoy's own family. Thus Natasha is partly his wife and partly her sister Tanya; Count Ilya Rostov is Tolstoy's grandfather, also called Ilya and also a great gourmet (his fish were especially shipped from the Black Sea); Nicholas Tolstoy, Tolstoy's father, appears as Nicholas Rostov. He also sought to repair the family fortunes. And he too married an heiress, Princess Mary Volkonskaya, who had as companion a Mademoiselle Hénissienne. And so on.

And to an extent it is true all writers do this; the extreme example is, of course, Proust. But a knowledge of Proust's life adds nothing to his book. All that we need is there in the novel. It is not there in *War and Peace*. Tolstoy is writing an epic, and it is this, his power to leave out and stride on, to refrain from explanations, that enables him to do so, to include all those chance encounters and episodes, glimpses of other lives of which real life is composed. There is an almost physical strength in Tolstoy that makes him, as he is himself aware, peculiarly fitted for epic, a power to fuse by sheer force of instinct, to simplify, not to worry about how things will connect, how this or that thread can be woven in—not to invent but to set things down quite simply as they happen (and nothing, we feel, is invented in *War and Peace*: it is Tolstoy who saw the soldiers bathing, the little girls stealing the plums). He had, in fact, a horror of invention, a puritanical horror as of something superfluous, of the same kind that he felt for luxury, for anything smacking of artifice, for the allurements of women's dress, for anything exceeding the muzhik's needs.

Tolstoy was too inescapable an artist to be made, as he might have been, a mere realist by this doctrine. What he gives us is never a photograph but rather a Delacroix. This is art snatched from the jaws of life: Tanya comes to stay at Yasnaya Polyana, Tolstoy attends her to her first ball; she comes again with her brother, bringing a party of friends, among them her cousin and childhood love Kuzminsky; the party also includes a certain Anatole whom the Tolstoys decide is a bad lot; Anatole is sent packing; Tanya falls in love with Tolstoy's brother, Sergei, to whom she becomes engaged; he breaks the engagement off and it is Tanya, despairing, refusing to eat, with three doctors in attendance, Tanya whom nothing can interest or arouse, dragging herself through the summer days but who at length revives and sings again in her pure contralto voice—to whom, when she talks of returning to Moscow, Tolstoy blusters: ' "What! . . . Why you are posing for your portrait!" '

We think of Proust, the asthmatic, sealed off in his soundproof room, writing of the hawthorns of his child-hood, writing as if already dead, of time past, time mis-spent, a book that only his impending death enables him to release, like the spirit from the flesh, and invest with the new and different life of art.

It may not add to Natasha to know that she is Tanya. It does add something to the late Natasha to know that she is Sonya, to know what Sonya was like and what Tolstoy demanded of a wife. This alone, in fact, enables us to decode Natasha married. (Significantly this weakness in the book occurs where he is writing of the person closest to him.) The late Natasha's behaviour, her lack of repose, her absorption in her children, capriciousness, jealousy, do not add up, thrown off the scent as we are by the artful manipulation, by Tolstoy's presentation of all this as the outward, if curious, signs of a happily married woman. We have only to meet Sonya to come to our senses, to realise that what he is actually, unconsciously depicting is a woman sexually unfulfilled.

This Natasha is not in fact Sonya. She is something else, a mixture, part what Tolstoy wanted her to be and part what he did not want but none the less created. It was not Sonya who insisted on breast-feeding; nor was it Sonya who on her marriage neglected her appearance, but

Tolstoy who demanded that she do so. If she altered her hair or changed her dress this was 'frivolous'. She felt like 'flirting with someone', 'going to a ball', 'kicking up my heels instead of going upstairs to bed'. 'I am surrounded by decrepitude.' Tolstoy's only reaction was to tell her, 'That's enough'. She on her side accused him of being a kill-joy. "You know Tanya," she said after listening the next morning to her sister's glowing account of her first ball, at which the Czar had been present but which, being unwell, Sonya had been unable to attend, "I could not have gone even if I had been well. Surely you know Lyvotchka's views. Could I dress in a ball-gown with an open neck? This is absolutely unthinkable. How often has he not condemned married women who 'go naked' as he expresses it!"

Deprived of her lively family and immured in the country, pregnant and with nothing to occupy her, Sonya did what she could. She set herself to master domestic matters. Still, as Tolstoy says, a mere child, scantily equipped for the role of mistress of Yasnaya Polyana by the life she had hitherto led in the happy-go-lucky Behrs family, she did not embrace the task with enthusiasm, as is plain from her diary. It was not that there was a lack of things to do 'but one must first discover a liking for those trifling matters—winding the clock . . . and pickling cucumbers'.

Tolstoy was neither sympathetic nor grateful for her efforts; he resented what he called 'this change in her', her concern with what he regarded as trivial material cares— cares which came to include their finances, their children (thirteen), the estate which he left entirely to Sonya, a

course not unusual in an artist nor of necessity blame·
worthy, but which, in the case of the Tolstoys, forged the
ground which led to their estrangement.

In the light of this it is moving to read Fet's description of her, the young Countess running at Tolstoy's
call, and, to Fet's horror—she is pregnant—leaping a
hedge, a heavy bunch of household keys jangling at her
waist.

It is moving and enlightening to come on this entry
made in her diary while Tolstoy was away: 'I live for him,
by him, and wish him to be the same'; without him, she
writes, the place is oppressive to her, 'And,' she continues,
'today I ran off. I could hardly keep from laughing out
loud for joy as I ran softly out of the house. . . . If I do
not absorb him, if I'm a doll, if I'm only a wife and
not a human being, then I cannot live so and do not wish
to . . .'

There exists an extraordinary document, a letter-cum-
story, written by Tolstoy six months after his marriage,
for the amusement of his sister-in-law, the fifteen-year-
old Tanya, and entitled *The Tale of the Porcelain Doll*. He
is writing, he says, to tell her and to ask her to prepare
and inform her parents that Sonya 'who, as you know, has
always been made of flesh and blood like the rest of us'
suddenly, one night, approaching the bed, became 'not the
Sonya you and I have known but a porcelain Sonya. . . .
You know those porcelain dolls. Sonya was like that. I
touched her arm, she was smooth, pleasant to feel and
cold porcelain. . . .' And suddenly 'she seemed to shrink,
as it were, and became tiny, smaller than the palm of my
hand'. The next day at lunch she was her normal self.

'But every time we are alone together the same thing happens. She suddenly becomes small and porcelain.'

The joke is strangely near the bone. In Sonya, the porcelain doll, we not only have a Sonya cold in bed, but Sonya forced into a mould, deprived of her spontaneity, a Sonya alien, no longer his equal or soul-mate but shrunk after six months of marriage to mere doll size, that is life size, her mind exclusively occupied with trivia.

The late Natasha is both Sonya the porcelain doll and also—this is worse—Sonya reformed, not Sonya as she is but as he would wish her to be. One's gorge cannot but rise at the thought of her copying these pages as she has copied all the rest. *The Porcelain Doll* contains two remarks easily passed over, the first when he speaks of Sonya 'having always been made of flesh and blood . . . with all the advantages and disadvantages of that condition', a remark of which one might well think no more were it not for the further one. In the presence of other people Sonya is normal but as soon as they are alone she becomes 'small and porcelain'. To this he adds: 'Strange as it may seem, I frankly confess I am glad of it and though she is porcelain we are very happy.'

In other words—has he not said it?—he wanted her to be porcelain and is glad that she has turned out a mere doll, thus fulfilling his savage conviction that all women are mere dolls. This is his revenge on the female sex for the desire they arouse in him. In Gorki's opinion Tolstoy hated women and loved 'to punish them', though whether due to their failure to satisfy him or 'to the hostility of the spirit to the degrading impulses of the flesh', Gorki could not decide. 'But it is hostility and cold.' Tolstoy wanted

his wife to be frigid but he also, as in everything, wanted
it both ways. During the time he was writing and she
copying *War and Peace* Sonya had borne Tolstoy four
children. When she asked on medical grounds for a respite
Tolstoy was furious. 'The strong, handsome and fertile'
later Natasha, who 'at the rare moments when the old fire
kindled in her handsome, fully developed body was even
more attractive than in former days', must strike us, at
least for the time at which it was written, as an oddly
coarse, indeed animal description. This then was to be
Sonya's reward, the lesson meted out at the end of her six
years of copying and re-copying *War and Peace*.

Does not the later Natasha strongly suggest a peasant
woman, the big blowzy Aksinia, for example, Tolstoy's
former mistress, whom Sonya, the bride, had encountered
scrubbing the floors at Yasnaya Polyana, by whom he had
had a son, she who, Sonya reflected with horror, had lain
like herself in Tolstoy's arms?

I have spoken of Tolstoy's style as peculiarly fitted for
epic. Oddly it is this same 'epic' style that engenders our
feeling of intimacy—there are omissions and there are
repetitions. We have the sense of Tolstoy telling us what
he knows himself, telling us as one does tell such things—
reiterating certain points, forgetting to mention others.
(Why as a boy did Pierre hate his father and want to run
away from home? What about Pierre's mother?) Verbally
he is extremely repetitive. He has no time, one feels, to
fuss about using the same word twice in a sentence. This
is not artlessness but art—not Turgenev's art, but to say
it is less polished would be unwise. How is it that if

A DARING COIFFEUR

Tolstoy repeats himself, the effect is not verbose, we do not feel the narrative impeded? What is said is not with Tolstoy dulled but sharpened by repetition. It does not lose but gains an added freshness. It gains, that is, in veracity. Most books are a form of sharp practice. They move faster than we think or can possibly remember. They may be said to 'pull a fast one on us'. With Tolstoy, on the other hand, we relax, we participate, we have the sense of his thinking out loud in our presence. It is this that allows us to feel so much at home in *War and Peace*, more at home, perhaps, than we do in life, more secure than since our childhood. With the entry of the late Natasha all is changed. We feel, on the contrary, insecure. In place of candour we have innuendo. The tone is forced, the tone of someone making a bad joke. Tolstoy is working very close to life, too close for comfort and, it must be faced, too close for art. 'Morality is hot but art is icy. Cool first, write afterwards.' Such was the advice of Henry James to the young Vernon Lee. James may be an extreme case, a writer for whom a little living went a mysteriously long way. Few writers have shared his immunity. Few, perhaps, had they done so would have written anything at all. Most artists are driven to what they do by life, by tensions they cannot resolve in other ways, frequently by despair. In this they are closer to Tolstoy than to James. But if James is an extreme case, Tolstoy is no less so. When radical critics objected that *War and Peace* did not properly portray either the misery of the peasants or the faults of the aristocracy, Tolstoy appears to side with James: 'The aims of art,' he wrote, 'are incommensurable with social aims. The aim of an artist is not to resolve a

question irrefutably, but to compel one to love life in all
its manifestations, and these are inexhaustible. If I were
told that I could write a novel in which I would indis-
putably establish as true my point of view on all social
questions, I would not dedicate two hours to such a work;
but if I were told that what I would write would be read
twenty years from now by those who are children today,
and that they would weep and laugh over it and fall in love
with the life in it, then I would dedicate all my existence
and all my powers to it.'

The paradox remains: he was to dedicate all his existence
and all his powers to denying these very words, to denying the value of earthly life, of tears, laughter, love, to
laying down the law and writing tracts, to what Gorki in
Nietzsche's phrase terms '"a negation of all affirmations".'
But Tolstoy's dogmatism is there from the start. It is
already present, as I have sought to show, in *War and
Peace*. Even when writing the passage I have quoted,
refusing to prostitute his art, he is already doing so. Even
when defending art from life, he does not, one feels, really
grasp in what the threat consists. 'Morality is hot but art is
icy.' Art and life, James is saying, are two different com-
partments. To Tolstoy with his cult of the instinctive,
his horror of 'clever folk', of what he deemed artifice, this
doctrine must have been anathema.

War and Peace is a great work but it is flawed by life,
by lack of detachment, hysteria, nostalgia. Its greatness is
hard to analyse. We feel it, but are uneasy. Why should
Tolstoy be greater than Henry James? Such classifications
are pointless and yet the question nags. We feel that
Tolstoy is greater. We dislike it. We do not find life

simple. We prefer Henry James. We do not like moralists and bullies.

It seems to me that *War and Peace* is flawed by being written too early, too close to what Tolstoy was himself living through. True, the events it describes are those of an earlier period. But just as we may ponder Tolstoy's title, may wonder whether *War and Peace* was not perhaps crystallised, touched off too early by marital difficulties, so we may wonder whether history was not itself useful to him. Not only did it entail vast research, a pretext for retiring for long hours to his study. History was a substitute for detachment. It was this that allowed him his idyll, that allowed him to minimise the pain of individual experience.

But wherever we turn with Tolstoy we are met by paradox. In some ways he is inhumanly detached.

It is this side of his nature that he himself depicts in Prince Andrew, the most Stendhalian character in the book, to my mind the most interesting and the hardest to understand. Whereas, despite his unheroic aspect, we early perceive that Tolstoy has a special weakness for Pierre, in other words that Pierre is to be our hero, we less readily accept the fact that he shares the role with Prince Andrew. The latter makes an unpleasant impression on us; that is, he is depicted in a way which makes us dislike him, which acts as a barrier to our understanding. Thus in the early scene with Lise, his wife, that takes place in the presence of Pierre, there is little doubt with whom our sympathies lie. Irritating and silly as she is, Lise's piteous appeal strikes home. We feel there is justice in it.

Moved by this and unpleasantly affected by the sudden cringing fear she betrays of her husband, we are little disposed to be moved by Prince Andrew's anguish, by his own subsequent desperate cry, ' "Never, never marry. . . ! "' We understand that Prince Andrew regrets his marriage. And we may recognise his discontent with triviality. This brings us no nearer to understanding Prince Andrew. We feel his exasperation but reject his attitude. We do not place ourselves in Prince Andrew's shoes. We are not, let us be plain, in the mood to understand him. Tolstoy himself is responsible for this. It is he who engenders our mood, that mood of which I have spoken, a special, youthful, trusting, joyous mood to which we surrender in the first half of *War and Peace*, a mood in which we enjoy the secure sense that good is white and bad is black. Ambiguities, doubts, are swept away by happiness that defies events, an irrefutable joy, the triumphal joy of the *Pastoral Symphony*.

Prince Andrew's outburst occurs, it is true, very early on, before this note can be said to be established. It succeeds the overture—Anna Scherer's soirée. Our ears still filled with the hubbub of new voices, Prince Andrew's outburst somehow fails to make its proper impact. The truth is that it comes too early for us. If it was Tolstoy's intention to unmask Prince Andrew, to expose him for a moment off his guard, the intention, it seems to me, misfires. We know him to be proud, cold, reserved. To penetrate this reserve we need to know him better. As it is, as in actual life, the effect on us of such revelations, such violence from a stranger, is rather to make us recoil than sympathise. The episode, moreover, is swiftly effaced from our minds by that which succeeds it, the evening at Dolokhov's, the terrifying bet and drinking on the window sill, a chapter in turn succeeded, overlaid by the rising theme, by the music we hear coming from the Rostovs where they are celebrating Natasha's name-day.

On reaching the end of *War and Peace*, we do not immediately cease to inhabit the world we have come to know so well. We continue to recall, to ponder, to speculate. One of the questions we find ourselves asking is what would Prince Andrew have thought of Natasha married? Would he have reacted as we react, as Denisov reacts? Could domestic life have made him happy? But then what, we are obliged to ask, would Natasha have been like? We try to picture her as Prince Andrew's wife. But we cannot; the feat is beyond us, for the reason that we only now discover—that we retain a strangely indistinct picture of the Prince. We do not really know what he was like. We do our best to conjure up 'that small proud man' whose *savoir-faire* Nicholas Rostov so admired. To us for much of the book he seems reduced to a mere witness, useful to Tolstoy as a connecting thread, as providing us with an entrée to the presence of the great, of the Kutuzovs, Bilibins and Arakcheevs.

It is true the device is effective. We greatly enjoy these sorties into the world outside and around our story and do not, as with Tolstoy's lectures, resent them as interruptions. Nevertheless they are not, perhaps could not be, integrated, interlocked with Prince Andrew's experience as in the case of a Nicholas or a Natasha.

His end, the conversion and death—all that is wishy-washy. Our verdict on this at least is unhesitating. We have seldom been less moved, and cannot bring ourselves to share Princess Mary's pained surprise that Natasha should so indecently soon be capable of putting forth fresh feelings. But then the question arises: were we meant to be moved? How cruel he was even on his death-bed, how selfishly preoccupied with enacting his own death, how unfeeling to his little son Nicholas.

And how gratuitously cruel, how hateful he was that day to Princess Mary over the little boy's clothing! And why on this occasion? Was it because of his meeting with Natasha, the painful stirrings of new life, the change taking place within him and an impatience with all that remained unchanged? Or because he did not love the child but felt only a sense of duty, because he was prevented from loving him by remorse for the death of Lise for which he unconsciously blamed the little boy for reminding him?

How obscure it all is. We feel that he is cruel, unlikeable and yet that Tolstoy likes him. But why does he like Prince Andrew? Because he is irrational? Yes, perhaps there is something of this in it. And, recalling the clothing incident, we begin ourselves to mellow. What are we making all the fuss about? In behaving as he does Prince Andrew is behaving no differently from Nicholas and Natasha. His cruelty is human, lifelike. And for a moment we may feel that now we are really getting behind the scenes, feeling if not fully grasping what lies behind the cruelty. Coming to life is painful for this man. May not further more careful reading prove similarly rewarding?

A moment's reflection serves to give us pause. Prince Andrew is not irrational. He is not of the same stuff of which Natasha and Nicholas are made. And our dislike of him returning, the probability is that we dismiss Prince Andrew from our minds.

If, however, as sometimes happens with books we have greatly enjoyed, though seldom perhaps with ones as long as this, we come to the end only to start again at the beginning; if, at least, we re-read *War and Peace* before we have entirely forgotten our first impressions of it, we can scarcely fail to be arrested by our changed reaction to Prince Andrew's outburst. We come to this passage as if we had never read it. In place of its failure to register due to our inability to connect or relate it to anything we know, it now leaps out of the frame, starts up at us from the page in a way that seems more accident than art. Our response to this passage has this in common with our earlier one—it affects us as out of place and out of key, as too personal, a cry breaking despite himself from Tolstoy. Had it occurred later in the book, there might have been some grounds for this interpretation. As it is, however much it startles, we are bound to face the fact that a cry of desperation, a personal cry, is unlikely to find its way into the second chapter of a lesser work even than *War and Peace*.

It is Prince Andrew's function here to sound the call to war. His tirade is too long to quote in full (that this should be so makes our failure to register it the odder). Its gist, though not its full savagery, may be acquired from extracts:

' "Never, never, marry, my dear fellow! That's my

advice. Never marry until you can say to yourself that you've done all you are capable of, or until you have ceased to love the woman of your choice and have seen her plainly as she is, or else you will make a cruel and irrevocable mistake. . . . You don't understand why I say this . . . but it's the whole story of life. You talk of Buonaparte and his career . . . but Buonaparte went step by step towards his goal. He was free, he had nothing but his aim to consider, and he reached it. But tie yourself up with a woman, and like a chained convict you lose all freedom! And all you have of hope and strength merely weighs you down and torments you with regret. Drawing-rooms, gossip, balls, vanity and triviality—these are the enchanted circle I cannot escape from. I am now going to the war, the greatest war there ever was, and I know nothing and am fit for nothing. I am very amiable [translation?] and have a caustic wit ... and at Anna Pavlovna's they listen to me. And that stupid set without whom my wife cannot exist, and those women. . . . If you only knew what those society women are, and women in general. My father is right. Selfish, vain, stupid, trivial in everything—that's what women are. . . ." '

It is easy now to see why we failed to grasp the significance and, as a result, mislaid this passage. We took it to be simply an attack on women. Prince Andrew's identification with his father, his words: 'My father is right', confirm this impression. The old Prince, a grandee of Catherine's reign, is himself a veteran soldier, a former field-marshal. Our subsequent meeting with the old Prince, the way in which Tolstoy presents him to us seated at his lathe, the geometry lesson, his treatment of

61

Princess Mary, his rules, his hours, his lack of ordinary understanding, his eccentricity, his despotism—all this leads us to think of him not as formed by life but rather as a natural phenomenon, a promontory against which life may beat itself in vain. Prince Andrew clearly is very like his father. He admires and emulates him. In both men, therefore, their attitude to women seems natural; we think of it as a part of their military baggage rather than as a motivating force.

It is as if with Prince Andrew, Tolstoy is bent on being ambiguous. Why does Prince Andrew like Pierre? We are told why Pierre likes Prince Andrew: 'He considered his friend a model of perfection just because he possessed in the highest degree the very qualities that Pierre lacked and which might best be described as strength of will.' Tolstoy goes on to enumerate the reasons why Pierre liked Prince Andrew. The other side of the friendship is less simple and Tolstoy does not explain it. We must make do with digs and innuendo. Thus 'Even', we read, 'in the best, simplest, most friendly relations . . . praise and commendation are essential just as grease is necessary to wheels that they may run smoothly.' A couple of sentences on from this we read that Prince Andrew looked kindly at Pierre 'yet his glance . . . expressed a sense of his own superiority'.

Prince Andrew then is flattered. He patronises Pierre. Moreover, the fact is everyone likes Pierre. Why? because he is guileless. Thus Lise does not speak to her husband as she does despite Pierre's presence; she speaks in this way *because* Pierre is there, because with Pierre it is pointless to pretend, because he is not—like her husband —clever or sarcastic, because the sudden sense that he is kind unmans her and unleashes her pent-up unhappiness. Similarly Prince Andrew does not confide his misery to Pierre simply because he is present, but because Pierre has seen how matters stand. Without this he might not have spoken; but nor, on the other hand, would he have spoken as he does to anyone else.

In fact, it is true that Prince Andrew is drawn to Pierre by pride; he is drawn to him by a moral fastidiousness in a world where almost everyone is jostling for place. It is pride that makes Prince Andrew cruel to Lise, pride that makes him honest, more honest than is common; to be otherwise would seem to him degrading. He would feel sullied by it. His honesty defeats his cleverness. It saves him from being, as he might have been, a second Bilibin. And allows him to value in Pierre a simplicity that he later meets and admires in a greater man—Kutuzov. It is partly this that makes us find him puzzling. The concept of the *honnête homme*, of this kind of self-respect, the thought that there may be anything good in pride, is wholly alien to us, hag-ridden as we are by our terror of appearing snobbish. Tolstoy's contemporaries would not have needed themselves to be aristocrats to understand Prince Andrew's motivation.

But, it may be objected, we understand Stendhal. If we can rise to a Julien Sorel whose acrobatic feats, surely, are far more dazzling (Prince Andrew does not go in for climbing ladders)—if we can manage Julien, why not Prince Andrew? Both men have the same exceptional gifts, the same desire for glory—without the same motives. It is partly this that makes Julien easier for us. The fact that he is of peasant stock with a coarse and brutal father, that in aspiring to a different kind of life, in making his way up he has continually to support the insults of those who are inferior to him, superior only by virtue of graft or wealth or birth; his desire to revenge himself on this society; the supremely aristocratic way in which, having done this, he sacrifices everything for love; all this, however alien, may be easily understood; the motives are clear, the development convincing.

Prince Andrew is not, in the same way, self-explanatory. We do not know the grounds of his need for glory. Disappointment with women, the need to stretch his wings? No, it is more complex, more confused, as appears from the passage where he is at his most explicit: alone with his thoughts on the eve of Austerlitz, with his fantasies of how, when all appears lost, 'he firmly and clearly expresses his opinion, to Kutuzov, to Weyrother, and to the Emperors. All are struck by the justice of his views, but no one offers to carry them out, so that he takes a regiment, a division . . .' and placing himself at the head of his troops it is he who gains the victory. Kutuzov remains commander in name only. A second victory follows. Kutuzov is dismissed and Prince Andrew is appointed in his place. So far this might be Julien Sorel. ' "If before that," the inner voice continues, "you are not ten times wounded, killed or betrayed!" "Well then," Prince Andrew answers himself, "I don't know what will happen, and I don't want to know and can't, but if I want this—want glory, want to be known to men, want to be loved by them, it is not my fault that I want it and want nothing but that and live only for that. Yes, for that alone! I shall never tell anyone, but oh God! what am I to do if

I love nothing but fame and men's love? Death, wounds, the loss of family—I fear nothing. And precious and dear as are many persons to me—father, sister, wife—those dearest to me—yet dreadful and unnatural as it seems, I would give them all at once for a moment of glory, of triumph over men, of love from men I don't know and never shall know!" '

The difference between Prince Andrew and Julien Sorel is at once apparent in the cry: ' " It's not my fault that I want it [glory] and want nothing but that . . . but oh God! what am I to do if I love nothing but fame . . . dreadful and unnatural as it seems" ' he would give them all—father, sister, wife—' "for a moment of glory . . . of love from men I don't know and never shall know".'

Julien is troubled by no such scruples but only by whether or not he can successfully seduce his employer's wife and, by this means, further his advancement. He does not waste time bemoaning his condition, but deliberately sets out to mould himself, to cultivate those aims that Prince Andrew sees as 'dreadful and unnatural'.

The two men are, in fact, poles apart. It may be worth saying something here of the nature of Stendhal's influence on Tolstoy. The latter first read Stendhal when in the army. What he read confirmed his experience at Sevastopol where he served on the terrible Fourth Bastion. Stendhal's debunking of battles and military leaders, his way of divesting them of their legendary qualities, was not only to serve Tolstoy as a precedent (Fabrizio on the field of Waterloo might have come straight out of the pages of *War and Peace*); Stendhal's presentation of war as chaos confirmed Tolstoy's own sceptical view of strategy, of the notion that battles can be planned, his contempt for military leaders. The decision on the part of the high command to abandon Sevastopol; the manner in which the garrison, left to perish, fought its way out; the spirit of the common soldiery, their cheerful, uncomplaining, humble spirit, left a never-to-be effaced impression on Tolstoy's mind. It was thus, paradoxically, Stendhal who contributed to the foundations of Tolstoy's cult of the peasant and his contempt for the aristocracy.

We are not, I have said, in the mood to understand Prince Andrew. My reasons for saying this may now appear more explicit. What is a Stendhalian character doing in *War and Peace*? Stendhal stands for wit, for worldliness. He should not be read, since he cannot be understood, when we are young. What is Prince Andrew doing then in this world, where if we read of war even, we read as children? Prince Andrew is an adult character. Few children would not be chilled, ill at ease with Prince Andrew. This is the ground of Tolstoy's quarrel with him. Prince Andrew has forgotten what it is like to be a child. He has nothing of the child left in him, nothing except, perhaps, a child's honesty. He is the only character in the book who, as we have said, is neither naïve nor corrupt. Nevertheless, as an adult it is fitting that he should be the one to sound the call to war: children do not make war, adults do. I have already drawn one, the obvious distinction between children and adults, the dividing line of puberty. There is also another division; children do not believe in their own deaths. Adults do. Their lives are lived in the presence of their deaths. And for each in his own way it is necessary to face and come to terms with death. Prince Andrew is best, perhaps only understood, in the context of this relationship. His story is a love affair with death. To say this is to indicate a degree of extremism. But we are not merely dealing with an adult—but with a particular adult: Tolstoy. Tolstoy is not an ordinary man; everything in him was outsize, carried to extremes; and *War and Peace* is no ordinary book. It is written very close in, near home. Not only are we unavoidably concious of Prince Andrew as Tolstoy's spokesman, since Tolstoy continually echoes him in the text; we do, I think, with Prince Andrew, feel that Tolstoy knows him too well to understand that we do not understand.

This in its turn is misleading. It implies that there is nothing special or difficult about Prince Andrew. This is not so. He is difficult. For all his characteristic sharpness of feature, the outline left in our minds is oddly ambiguous. Prince Andrew to us, at least, is an odd case. The fact is he appears before us in disguise. Prince Andrew is not a soldier but a monk.

Other words now come back to us, words lost on us at the time. And once again it is the same occasion, that of his desperate outburst to Pierre. Parting with his friend at the end of the evening Prince Andrew exhorts him to give up frequenting ' ". . . those Kuràgins. . . . It suits you so badly all this debauchery."

' "What would you have, my dear fellow?" answered Pierre shrugging his shoulders. "Women, my dear fellow; women!"

' "I don't understand it," replied Prince Andrew.

A DARING COIFFEUR

"Women who are *comme il faut*, that's a different matter. But the Kuràgins' set of women . . . I don't understand." '

This is the same man who only a little while earlier has been expressly denouncing society women: ' ". . . If you only knew what those society women are . . ." '

What are we meant to understand from this? Simply that Tolstoy wishes to bring in the concept '*comme il faut*'. Readers of *Youth* will remember the chapter devoted to this method of classifying his fellow human beings, to 'what has been one of the most pernicious and fallacious ideas with which society inoculated me'. How one spoke French or bowed, the arrangement of one's rooms, whether one had long, clean, well-kept nails, 'but above all the relation of his boots to his trousers', established a man as common or well bred. It was, he goes on, strange that he who had a positive incapacity for being *comme il faut* should have been so attracted by this conception. Young, painfully self-conscious, an aristocrat, obsessed by the conviction of his own ugliness, it does not surprise us that Tolstoy himself succumbed to this, the easiest way of asserting his superiority. Its importance was instilled in him by the aunt to whom the Tolstoy children were consigned in 1840, after the death of their other aunt and guardian. Polina Ilynishna Uskov was a *grande dame* moving in the highest social circles; 'It was this kind aunt with whom I lived (herself the purest of women)' who 'always told me that she desired nothing so much for me as an intimacy with a married woman. "*Rien ne forme un homme comme une liason avec une femme comme il faut . . .*"' (*Tolstoy's Confessions*).

Poor Polina's schemes for her nephew went sadly awry
—she intended him to be aide-de-camp to the Emperor.
The truth-telling of Tolstoy's *Sevastopol Sketches* effectively defeated her best efforts. Far from producing a
courtier, Polina did much to create Tolstoy, the anarchist,
in his peasant blouse.

In making Prince Andrew speak as he does, Tolstoy is
making him resume the mask of his urbanity. The language none the less seems to me to an extent private.
Tolstoy is having a hit at Polina's world, a hit he understands, but the point of which, in this context, we as
readers do not necessarily take.

Something of a similar sort occurs with the doctor's
wife who, travelling in her queer hooded vehicle—
carriage-cum-cart-cum-calèche—and caught up in the
retreat, shrieks out: ' "M.Aide de camp, M.Aide de camp!
. . . for heaven's sake protect me." ' An officer in charge
of a convoy is beating her driver for trying to get ahead of
the other vehicles. Prince Andrew intervenes on her
behalf. The officer defies him and says he will flatten him
into a pan-cake. ' "That was a nice snub for the little aide-
de-camp", ' came a voice from behind. Prince Andrew
sees that his championship of the woman in her queer trap
'might expose him to something he dreaded more than
anything else in the world—to ridicule'. Despite this he
persists and procures the woman's passage.

Later, restored to his unit, one of his friends, Prince
Nesvitskey, discussing the arrangements for the retreat
says . . . ' "But what's the matter . . .? You must be ill to
shiver like that." ' He has noticed Prince Andrew wincing
'as at an electric shock'. ' "It is nothing," replied Prince

Andrew. He had just remembered his recent encounter with the doctor's wife and the convoy officer.'

The episode, its effect on Prince Andrew, strike us as so strange, that we tend perhaps to make too much of it, to make mountains out of molehills, mysteries where none exist. What is the meaning of this episode? Why, we ask with shocked surprise, should Prince Andrew so fear ridicule? Such fear does indeed make him ridiculous.

The effect of this incident on him may in part, perhaps, be explained by the fact that a woman has involved him in it. It is this that Prince Andrew holds against women— their power to degrade. All contact with them is to him degrading.

I have already given one reason why Tolstoy felt in this way: the degree of desire aroused in him by women, his inability to reconcile the animal side of his nature with his other 'higher' mental side. This motivation cannot be extended to Prince Andrew, but its concomitant or contributory cause can—Tolstoy's disappointment with women, his not unnatural failure to find an equal; his cult, in women especially, of those who had not yet exchanged their youth for mundane, in his eyes 'trivial', preoccupations.

How much of human activity seems to Prince Andrew trivial—ordinary life with its pleasures and affections, the hunting enjoyed by Nicholas and Natasha, for example (pleasures available to him on his estates, no less than to the Rostovs). Driving him through a forest in the spring the coachman cannot refrain from turning on the box: ' "How pleasant it is your Excellency" he said. "What?" "It's pleasant, your Excellency!" "What is he talking about?" thought Prince Andrew. "Oh yes, the spring, I suppose", he thought as he turned round. "Yes, everything is green already. . . ." '

The love of women, the beauty of nature, all this means nothing to him. Oddly the event that affects him most is the death of Lise, a wife from whose company in life he had sought only to escape. But before going on it may be worth returning to the passage which precedes the affair of the doctor's wife. In it Tolstoy describes how Prince Andrew 'looked with disdain at the endless confused mass of detachments . . . overtaking one another and blocking the muddy road'. The shouting, the dead horses by the wayside, some flayed; 'the broken-down carts beside which solitary soldiers sat waiting . . . soldiers floundering knee-deep in mud'; while 'the voices of the officers directing the march . . . were but feebly heard amid the uproar'.

Surveying this struggling, pitiful mass of humanity in distress, Prince Andrew feels no compassion, only disdain. And one recalls Gorki's description of Tolstoy: 'I often thought him to be a man who in the depths of his soul is stubbornly indifferent to people; he is so much above and beyond them that they seem to him like midges and their activities ridiculous and miserable. He has gone too far away from them into some desert, and there, solitary with all the forces of his spirit, he closely examines into "the most essential", into death.'

It might have been thought that the death of Lise would come as a release, would at most inspire a temporary remorse. Instead it inspires a far more lasting sense of futility. Life becomes completely pointless to him. He leaves the army and retires for three years to his estates. For a moment, with the entry of Natasha, a desire for life briefly flickers into being. But his rendezvous has always been with death. To desire fame and glory is to opt for posthumous life. It is the Christian's rejection of this world in favour of life hereafter. It is a religious outlook, but profane, unredeemed by a faith in God or by the love of God. Prince Andrew is the stuff of which saints are made, the uncomfortable stuff of a Simone Weil, a saint without a God. But as always it is Gorki who puts it best:

'He reminds one of one of those pilgrims who all their life long, stick in hand, walk the earth travelling thousands of miles from one monastery to another, from one saint's relics to another, terribly homeless and alien to all men and things. The world is not for them, nor God either. They pray to Him from habit, and in their secret soul they hate Him; why does He drive them over the earth from one end to the other? What for? People are stumps, stones, roots on the path; one stumbles over them and sometimes is hurt by them.'

A sense of life as arid is not, of necessity, the concomitant of extraordinary powers. It is simply life rendered arid by the fear of death, an inability to relish life, to enjoy the passing hour, to surrender to the moment because one cannot forget that one must die.

Prince Andrew's thoughts before Austerlitz and his 'new' thoughts on his death-bed, reveal a striking similarity. What is the difference between Prince Andrew's desire for glory, 'for the love of men I don't know and never shall know' (as opposed to those he does know, love for whom entails all the irritations of reality), the view he has held throughout most of life as trivial, and that which he now expresses on his death-bed? 'To love everything and everybody and always to sacrifice oneself for love meant not to love anybody, *not to live this earthly life* [my italics]. And the more he became imbued with that principle of love, the more he renounced life and the more he destroyed that dreadful barrier [i.e., particular love], which stands between life and death. When during those first days he remembered that he would have to die, he said to himself ' "Well, what of it? So much the better." '

Much of Tolstoy's work seems in a curious way less to relate than to prognosticate.

I have emphasised the peculiarly autobiographical nature of a great deal of Tolstoy's work. Often, however, as other critics have not been slow to remark, this takes the form not merely of recollection but of what seems an almost uncanny, terrifying clairvoyance; less an analysis of what has been than a prognostication of what is yet to come. And it is possible, like Gorki, to ask the question: How if he saw all this, if he saw himself so clearly—and Gorki was convinced that he did see—how was it that he continued to behave as he did? Why, if he saw that such and such was wrong, was a weakness in himself, did he continue to indulge it? At the time of writing *War and Peace* Tolstoy was still taking an active part in family life, joining in the young people's theatricals and playing the piano for Tanya. Later, such home-made pleasures on the part of his own children made him furious; they were frivolous and trivial. Prince Andrew then is not so much an aspect of Tolstoy himself. He is what Tolstoy was later to become.

Everyone carries within himself the seeds of his later self. And this view may be more or less depressing. It is possible, it seems to me, that Tolstoy was formed too early for any subsequent knowledge or self-awareness to unmake what was already made. Tolstoy's mother died when he was two; his father dropped dead in the street seven years later; this same year the children, absorbed in their favourite game of making fires in their chamber-pots, were interrupted by the tutor bearing news of their grandmother's death. The aunt to whose charge they were then consigned died within two years. In both *Childhood* and *Family Happiness* Tolstoy stresses the numbness of grief, the agreeable sense of self-importance induced by being an orphan, his efforts to look tragic. In other words his feelings lacked an outlet. The death, when Tolstoy was twenty-eight, of his younger brother Dmitri, probably served as a model for the death from consumption of Levin's brother. It was followed by that of his favourite elder brother and hero, Nicholas, also from T.B., Nicholas whom some thought more gifted than Tolstoy, the being who Tolstoy most loved, and who died in his arms.

At the time of writing *War and Peace* Tolstoy had not yet experienced what for the rest of his life he was to call 'the fear of Arzamas'—the terrible experience partly engendered, perhaps, by what today we would call a nervous breakdown after *War and Peace*, an experience of suffocating horror, of meeting the spectre of death, which overtook him one night when putting up at an inn at Arzamas.

The experience, however, was surely no more than the climax, the outbreak of the long-suppressed child's horror. In a letter to Fet he described how Nicholas 'some moments before his death drowsed off, but suddenly . . . awoke and whispered with horror, "What is that?" That was when he saw it—the absorption of himself into nothingness.'

This episode is echoed in Prince Andrew's dream of pushing with all his weight against a door from the other side of which something, which it suddenly dawns on him is Death itself, is trying to break in.

For some time after the death of his brother, Tolstoy shared Prince Andrew's sense of futility after Lise's death. He too, as Prince Andrew puts it to Pierre on the ferry, had 'looked in', into that nothingness where someone has been. Nothing seemed to him either worth doing or writing. In the letter I have quoted to Fet, he goes on: 'One must somehow use the strength that remains to one. But as soon as a man reaches the highest degree of development, then he clearly sees that it is all nonsense and deceit, and that the truth—which he loves better than all else—is terrible. And when you look at it well and clearly you awake with a start and say with terror, as my brother did: "What is that?" Of course so long as the desire to know and speak the truth exists, one tries to know and speak. That alone remains to me of the moral world; higher than that I cannot place myself. That alone I will do, only not in the form of your art. Art is a lie and I can no longer love a beautiful lie.'

I have said that *War and Peace* is a great work flawed

by life. Should one not rather say it is flawed by death?
The sense of futility expressed in his letter to Fet was not
the symptom of a passing grief. It was to dominate and
embitter his whole personal life. As an old man himself
nearing death, it produced the remark recorded by Gorki
' "What is the use of truth, since knowing it a man must
still die?" '

Thirty-seven years after his repudiation of art in favour
of truth as expressed in his letter to Fet, the same sense of
futility produced *What is Art*, the question framed as
what is the use of art? Writing of de Maupassant, he tells
us that the latter had unhappily been brought up to
believe 'that life consists in pleasure and that the greatest
pleasure is to be found in woman and her love. . . . All
this might be well, but on examining these pleasures other
quite different things emerge, alien and hostile to this love
and this beauty. Woman for some reason is disfigured,
becomes unpleasantly pregnant and repulsive, gives birth
to children, unwanted children; then come deceptions,
cruelties, moral suffering, then mere old age and ultimately death.' If only one could arrest the relentless course
of life ' . . . but life goes on, and what does that mean?
Life goes on means that the hair falls out, turns grey, there
are wrinkles and offensive breath.' Even before this 'everything becomes dreadful, disgusting: the rouge, the powder,
the sweat, the smell and the repulsiveness, are evident. . . .'

What then, as Tolstoy was later to put it, *must we do?*
Turn away from life to the love of God? But no creed,
whether Catholic, Orthodox or Tolstoyan, can change
the unseemly way we are begotten, the unsightly way we
are born, the unattractive way we lose our teeth, go grey

and at last die. Far from loving God Tolstoy, moreover, says Gorki, hated Him. Gorki likens Tolstoy, as I have quoted, to those pilgrims 'terribly homeless and alien to all men and things. The world is not for them, nor God either. They pray to Him from habit and in their secret souls they hate Him.' Elsewhere, still more percipiently, perhaps, he compares Tolstoy and God to two bears in one den. What has Tolstoy got against God? Partly, he is jealous. God has done better. Gorki speaks of Tolstoy's despotic desire to impose his ideas, if need be to seek martyrdom to do so. 'This in him', he says, 'always repelled me, for I cannot help feeling that it is an attempt to use violence on me—a desire to get hold of my conscience. . . .' A further reason for Tolstoy's outlook is supplied by Gorki when he speaks of Tolstoy's nihilism 'sprung from the soil of an infinite and unrelieved despair . . . a loneliness which probably no one but he has experienced with such terrifying clearness'. We may include a further ground for resentment—his disappointment with women: the latter are not what they seem from a distance. They are deceivers, mere ordinary mortals. Reality disappoints—it does not equal the imagination.

So long as we enjoy life we do not ask, 'What is the use?' Natasha is untroubled by this question. When in the midst of her singing Prince Andrew hears her break off and leaning out on the moonlit balcony above him exclaim: ' "Oh God! Oh God! What does it mean?" ' Natasha's is the question posed by art, the question that needs no answer. (Whereas morality, unlike art, is the question posed and answered.)

It is the sense of futility, despair, that begets thinkers; the need to find a pattern, a meaning in life. And this takes us back to Prince Andrew; forward to Pierre Bezhukov. Both Tolstoy's heroes are unhappy; both ask 'What is the meaning of life?' They ask Natasha's question, but, unlike her, seek an answer to it. And this brings us full cycle to Tolstoy's central figure. Why does Tolstoy make Pierre his hero? Pierre is invariably clumsy, a slightly absurd figure. He is stout, bespectacled, unpolished. But this is itself a recommendation. Pierre is the glorification of the man whom society cannot corrupt. For society can only corrupt. This is what *War and Peace* is about. This is why Tolstoy prefers to pass his time with children, with Nicholas, Sonya, Boris and Natasha. We are back at the Rostovs: ' "Quick, what shall we sing?" ' But where is Sonya? Sobbing on the trunk, the place of mourning for female members of the Rostov family. Nicholas does not love her; yes he does. And, radiance restored, back we rush downstairs, back into that world of which Pierre is hero, since he has never lost the *naïveté* Tolstoy prizes, since he has never ceased to be a child.

It is true that Pierre is well known to lead a life of dissipation, that he is always resolving to give this up but does not manage to do so. When during his initiation into the Freemasons he is asked to name his chief passion, 'that passion which', as his questioner puts it, 'more than all others has caused him to depart from the path of virtue', he replies, ' "Women".' But since we are shown none of this side of his life, since we are not only never allowed to witness these orgies but do not even see their aftermath; since we never see him behaving irritably with servants or even feeling ill with a hangover; since he appears, on the contrary, to enjoy excellent health and, in the bargain, for all his so-called repentance, what to most of us would seem an enviably cloudless conscience, we simply continue with our child's role; that is to say we read as we read when we were children, ignoring what we do not understand.

The fact that we do not believe in Pierre's debauchery, that his repentance, too, seems to us unreal, since it includes none of that convulsive self-disgust which must surely accompany such repentance—oddly this does not trouble us, does not make Pierre himself less real. If we reflect, a reason occurs to us. Is it not this—that Tolstoy intends us to feel in this way, that he anticipates our attitude, that he is himself treating Pierre's repentance as unreal, even, going one better, as slightly absurd? No, after all, it is all all right. We are safely on child's ground. There is nothing of which we need to be afraid.

One difficulty arises. Pierre's attitude is unworldly; we may at times find ourselves disconcerted, unprepared for his honesty. His reaction after the duel with Dolokhov, for example, may well disarm us. ' "But in what was I to blame?" he asked. "In marrying her without loving her; in deceiving yourself and her." And he vividly recalled that moment after supper at Prince Vasili's, when he spoke those words he had found so difficult to utter: "I love you. It all comes from that! Even then I felt . . . I had no right to do it. And so it turns out." '

No one has suggested to Pierre that he is in the wrong. On the contrary, he is the one who has been wronged. And yet his first, his only instinct, is to blame himself.

How is it possible that such a man, capable of such fairness, himself leading the life of a debauchee whose admitted weakness is women, should have behaved as he did towards a wife still aged only nineteen? Would he not, as a fellow-sinner, rather have sought to help than repudiate and abandon her? The truth is it is not her unfaithfulness that makes him leave Helène. He is repelled by her sexuality; the more so since he himself took advantage of it during the first weeks of their honeymoon. He is filled with shame by the memory of being caught by his steward coming out of his wife's bedroom at midday.

He recoils from Helène not as unfaithful but as impure. He would much have preferred her to be frigid. Tolstoy's whole treatment of her is significant. Helène is a grotesquely simplified figure, never treated in depth. Tolstoy, plainly, is terrified of her charms. So little, indeed, is he prepared to have any truck with her, to make her anything more than a cardboard dummy, that he does not even trouble to describe her differently. We are saddled with her white arms and bosom, so invariably saddled that we are reminded of Homer's epithets, his 'grey-eyed Athené', and his 'wine-dark sea'. Is not Helène's name itself, in fact, an unconscious echo, a short-cut to her role in Tolstoy's epic?

To understand Tolstoy's weakness, his attitude to women and his choice of Pierre as a hero, it is necessary, at least, to take into account the aristocratic society to which he belonged. Why is Russian boredom the epitome of boredom? Because of the remoteness of the estates; because of the Russian winter, of the vast pine forests?

WAR AND PEACE

We think of a *Month in the Country*, of *Uncle Vanya*. There is less boredom in *War and Peace*, for good reason—there is War. But, even so, Natasha is constantly bored, constantly idle. It never enters her head to read a book. Despite a French-speaking aristocracy, Russia was not included in the Grand Tour. Why? Because it possessed little art, because it was not a place in which culture was to be gained, because its people were barbarians. Pierre has been educated abroad. Four years in Paris have left him as clueless as if he had been in the Hebrides; to us, he remains, as does Tolstoy himself, essentially the product of the society Tolstoy vilifies.

Pierre is the anti-hero, the philistine as hero. He is Tolstoy's indictment of this society. A rich man, he also embodies Tolstoy's sense of futility. Significantly we notice that it is war that gives Pierre his first taste of happiness: '"If only,"' we recall Prince Andrew exclaiming, '"if only everything were as simple as it seems to Mary."' A prisoner-of-war, suffering extreme hardship, Pierre feels 'a glad consciousness that everything that constitutes men's happiness, the comforts of life, wealth, *even life itself* [my italics] is something it is pleasant to throw away—compared with something . . . with what?'

If only things could be other than they are. If only men need not grow up, if only there were no sex, if only life were not so complicated. And Tolstoy rounds on us, baring his teeth at all that is complicated, damning it out of hand as insincere.

His tragic inability to accept the sexual instinct, to accept the full implications of adult life, led him to reject his own complexity. This rejection culminates in Pierre. And since he cannot ultimately take things as they are, cannot accept the diversity of life in its sexual, its humdrum, its mixture of good and bad aspects, we are left not with a Pierre, strengthened, as he might have been, by contact with a harsher side of life than is commonly open to his class—we are left with a nonentity. Rich, influential, had he wished to be so, particularly well-equipped, one would have thought, to perform a useful function as leader at a time when the dissolution of serfdom created a special need for enlightenment in the aristocracy, Pierre parts from us still weak, still absorbed in Utopian schemes. The most we can say of him is that he does no harm.

'But', says Henry James in an essay on Turgenev, 'the world is no illusion, no phantasm, no evil dream of a night; we wake up to it again for ever and ever; we can neither forget it, nor deny it, nor dispense with it. We can welcome experience as it comes, and give it what it demands, in exchange for something about which it is idle to pause to call little or much, so long as it contributes to swell the volume of consciousness. In this there is mingled pain and delight, but over the mysterious mixture there hovers an invisible rule, that bids us learn to will and seek to understand.'

But Tolstoy—has he not said it?—is against understanding. 'A Russian', he himself writes, 'is self-assured because he knows nothing and does not want to know anything, since he does not believe that anything can be known.' He contrasts this outlook favourably with German dogmatism.

The aperçu, if true of Tolstoy himself, is certainly true of Chekov. It is no less true of Dostoevsky. And yet, what we have is somehow something very different here. Let us first look briefly at Dostoevsky. Dostoevsky's version of the Russian attitude, the belief that it is impossible to know, is precisely what allows him to admit the coexistence, the inextricable mixture of good and evil; so that we may paradoxically speak of his 'innocence', picturing, in fact, what might be termed an 'inclusive' innocence, where Tolstoy's is 'exclusive'. Similarly with Chekov's characters. The questions they ask themselves resemble Natasha's questions; they are questions that remain unanswered, thrown up like so many tiny glimmering balls against the night, against the background of the universe; questions that do not seek to wrest the truth from God, that, with whatever degree of desperation, accept the unknown—it forms an essential part of their cogitations. What do I feel? Why do I feel as I do? What does it mean? What is the point, the meaning of my life? Somehow their questions are better than an answer, better because the scale is better, the diminutive scale of the figure silhouetted against the dark.

'A Russian is self-assured because he knows nothing.' Dostoevsky and Chekov, unlike Tolstoy, do not fear the unknown; they do not fear to see their questions glimmer, flicker a moment and die, extinguished by the darkness. Whereas Tolstoy is frightened of the dark. He does not want to know, since nothing can be known. This is simply the stork's attitude. But, at the same time, he wants it both ways. He not only asks: What is the meaning of life; not only does he ask; he actually, in the bargain, wants to determine the answer in advance.

And yet how queer, how unnecessary it seems, the misunderstanding! Pierre Bezhukov, the philistine as hero and Isabel Archer heroine of *Portrait of a Lady*, have after all sprung from a single cell; Tolstoy and Henry James, at opposite points of the compass (Tolstoy would have loathed James's work) both passed their lives asking: What is the use of culture? Can it be said to make men any better? Pierre Bezhukov is Tolstoy's answer, his answer to Gilbert Osborne, to *The Ambassadors*, to *The Europeans*, to the theme running throughout James's work. James poses the question very strongly. I have already given his answer (implicit, too, in his work). Against it we may fairly set the following, a letter from Tolstoy written to the young Romain Rolland:

'In our depraved society—the society of so-called civilised people—... the simplest and shortest ethical precept is to be served by others as little as possible and to serve others as much as possible.... This is what involuntarily drives a moral and honest man to prefer manual labour to the sciences and the arts; the book I write, for which I need the work of the printer; the symphony I compose for which I need the work of musicians ... the picture I paint for which I need the work of those who manufacture pigments and canvas— all these things can be useful to men, but they can also be—and are, for the most part—utterly useless and even harmful. And while I am doing all these things whose usefulness is highly questionable ... there are an endless

number of things to do right in front of me, all of which
are undubitably useful . . . a burden to carry for someone
who is tired, a field to work for its owner who is ill, a
wound to dress . . . planting a tree, raising a calf, clearing
a well, are actions which are incontestably useful to others
and an honest man cannot fail to prefer them to the
dubious occupations which are proclaimed by our society
to be man's highest and most noble callings.'

It does not seem to occur to Tolstoy that there may
be times when we need something more complex done
for us, when such practical ministrations may merely
have the effect of leaving us to shoulder our real problems,
of stressing our isolation. How little, he seems to be
saying, one man can do for another—he can clean his well,
that is all. It is a loveless doctrine, a loveless world; a
world in which, unlike James's, there is little communi-
cation. Pierre Bezhukov gives us a poor answer.

And yet, as I have already said, how strange, how
small is the gulf; how absurd, in fact, the misunderstanding. For what, after all, is culture but an adult's
game? The game we continue to play by means of which
we deliver ourselves from earning a living and getting
a meal on the table. What is the end of culture but to
preserve the child's freedom of spirit, the child's advantages—freedom to enjoy the life of the mind, to revive
and nourish the life of the imagination, untrammelled by
arrangements and adult burdens? To shed our artificial,
preconceived notions and recover a freshness in ourselves.
To reach the state epitomised by Tolstoy in Pierre
Bezhukov? But Pierre is an utterly feeble character.
He is, let us face it, no substitute for James's Lambert

Strether. Moreover *War and Peace* is not the answer.
It leaves us with unconquerable feelings of irritation.
'But', says E. M. Forster, 'an unpleasant and unpatriotic
truth has here to be faced. No English novelist is as
great as Tolstoy.'

Why? In what does the greatness consist? It consists
in this; that Tolstoy is like a man out of hospital. If you
yourself have ever passed a term in hospital where everything is clean and above all white, and emerged to be
driven away, anywhere, out of the town, into the country,
it does not matter where, everything—a barrow-boy with
a fruit stall on the corner, a blonde child, poplars, a woman
pushing a pram, everything strikes you as if you had
never seen such things. You feel that you will remember
them all your life. You climb into bed at home—for you
have still to rest—and everything, the ticking of the
clock, all those objects, pieces of furniture you would
have thought familiar to the point of invisibility, introduce themselves to you one by one in a way that strikes
you as extraordinarily friendly of them.

So it was always with Tolstoy—hence our happiness.
Everything he saw was at once natural, ordinary and
refreshingly vivid. Thus a soldier has only to put on his
boots or take them off to assume an absorbing interest for
us. But then Tolstoy is fresh from something more than
a mere sojourn in hospital. He is a man newly reprieved
from death, who hourly escapes from it. The very blight
that corroded his life and work must also be given its
due as the source of his singular power. It seems a hideous
treadmill of a circle; for must not the very vitality, the
heightened appetite for life with which nature had en-

dowed him, itself have trebled the meaning, the horror and the fear of death?

It is the fullness with which this man lived, his eye for the essential, the style which enabled him to make us see the world through his eyes, that places him head and shoulders above all other novelists. Ultimately life defeats death. Ultimately the artist defeats the moralist. Ultimately, then, we take leave of Tolstoy as he himself writes of the oak tree, the oak tree in the wood that Prince Andrew, driving past it, takes for dead. Everything else is green. Only the oak is leafless, ancient, hoary, joyless and forbidding. Later, returning this way, Prince Andrew looks for the oak tree. He looks at it without recognising it. The oak tree is transfigured. Luxuriantly covered now with foliage, it stands glittering, trembling in the evening sunlight: 'Neither gnarled fingers, nor old scars, nor old doubts or sorrows were any of them in evidence now. Through the hard, century-old bark, even where there were no twigs, leaves had sprouted such as one would hardly believe the old veteran could have produced.'

ON ANNA KARENINA

LREADY, as I have related, six years before his marriage Tolstoy had written *Family Happiness*. This book has a terrifying premonitory quality, perhaps a determining attitude to the future.

The title carries an irony. The book does not set out to give a picture of *Family Happiness*. The title refers to a man's dream of attaining such happiness. In fact no sooner are the lovers married than the dream fades, as it is bound to do. It has been replaced by reality. In both the two intertwined strands of *Anna Karenina* Tolstoy returns to this early theme.

His own words, recorded by Sonya, are too extra-ordinary not to be worth setting down here:

'In *Anna Karenina*,' he said, 'I love the idea of the family. In *War and Peace* I loved the idea of the people. In my next book I shall love the idea of the nation as a rising force.'

The idea of the nation as a rising force is a concept we find hard to love. 'My next book' was never written. But here too, even, Tolstoy — as so often — strikes us as prophetic. Of these generalisations it is not hard to say which is likely to make the better book. All three suggest missions, but that which sticks closest to persons, furthest from theories and factions, is the first.

It is worth noting Tolstoy's words and also worth noting the opening sentence of *Anna Karenina*: 'All

happy families are alike but an unhappy family is unhappy after its own fashion.'

It is probable that the reverse of this observation is
true. All descend into the same pit. Happy families are
rare—as happiness is rare, its propagation an unremit-
ting art. Adjective and noun, perhaps, cannot be coupled
today. Possibly Tolstoy is talking about something,
referring to an entity we have ceased to understand,
living in a—it may be—transitory phase when the gulf
between generations is cultivated, not bridged. But—let
us pause: he is not talking about it. We catch no single
glimpse of a happy family. Even Levin's brother-in-law,
Lvov, reading his little boy's grammar in order to try
to help him, says Levin's view of his children is idealised.
No family life is happy except, perhaps, Kitty's, but
her happiness makes her pedestrian. She, like Natasha,
becomes a milch-cow, polished off to a realm where
she, too, ceases to be human. No wonder that Levin's
sense of isolation is such that he is driven to contemplate
suicide.

This, in fact, is a book about human isolation, inter-
locking human isolations. The totality of this isolation
is such that all relationships within it even are a form of
torture; they are merely a jarring on, an intrusion, an
infringement of one isolation by another.

And yet it is true that the book, despite its subject-
matter, opens on a great wave of happiness—the irrepressible happiness of Stepan Arkadyevitch (it is easy to
shut the door on Dolly), of Levin with his lover's hopes.
It is a bachelor lunch; we are carried away by the sense
of our well-being. This we feel is what life should be like!

We feel it as we tuck in our starched napkins, reflecting that we have never liked oysters and how unwell we shall be for days after eating such a meal. This is what it is to be, as we are far from being, in a right relation to the world! The sheer goodness of life emerges from these pages like the smell of freshly baked bread. Yet Levin, and Oblonsky too, are isolated; each disapproves of the other. But this is smoothed over by Stiva's imperturbable good humour. His charm is an infectious quality. We ourselves fall on his neck when he comes to shoot with Levin. We have never been better pleased to see a guest. We open the book with him waking on the sofa in his study. He has been dreaming of little decanters like women on tables made of glass which sang *Il Mio Tesoro*—no, not that, perhaps *O Sole Mio*. . . .

The point I am making here, is that Oblonsky, the roué, is the only happy person in the book. And how, we may ask, does he contrive to achieve happiness? 'The answer is . . . live from day to day; in other words forget, but as he could not find forgetfulness in sleep, at least not until bedtime, nor return to the music sung by the little decanter women, he must therefore lose himself in the dream of life.'

To this extent, no more, Stepan Arkadyevitch may be said to prepare the way for Anna. But no, there is one other sentence. He is thinking of his unfaithfulness, of Dolly. ' "No she will never forgive me—she cannot forgive me. And the worst of it is that I am to blame for everything—I am to blame and yet I am not to blame. That is the whole tragedy," he mused.'

This is an adult tragedy, by which I do not mean that

A DARING COIFFEUR

Stepan Arkadyevitch is himself adult; but merely that when we are adult there is no one else to blame. We are both to blame and not to blame. We are what we have unconsciously, unthinkingly become. Not only are we not in control—we are no longer, as youth assumes, allowed the illusion of being so. The very qualities which go to make the enjoyment of Stepan Arkadyevitch are the identical qualities which create Anna's suffering.

The very buoyancy which has enabled Anna to survive her marriage to Karenin has allowed her to come through life too easily, without a struggle, without developing strength of character. She has lacked the compulsive streak which forges such a strength. She is, without being aware of it, rudderless. Moreover, all her life she has lacked passionate love. She has never been adored by her parents. She had none. Is this her fault? What woman in a similar position would not be conquered by such love, tenderness, passion, as Vronsky's?

If we stand back and pause with Matvey, his valet, to admire the blooming form of Stepan Arkadyevitch, inhaling the smell of coffee and fresh croissants, we may experience something of that same nostalgia which Tolstoy plainly felt for the social world, viewed not as in *War and Peace* as brutal and depraved but rather as if looking back on childhood—to a world where people were still, as he, Tolstoy, had once been, content to be thus childishly occupied, absorbed, their trivial lives unshadowed by thoughts of death. Some clue to the reason why Tolstoy chose to write, to identify with *Anna*, is provided by the chapter describing Levin's visit to the club—where people leave their troubles behind with their hats in the hall, where everyone is accepted and relaxed. We smell the leather chairs and feel the relief of it all, of this milieu where no women are admitted, where time and money are gambled away, where we see—can it really be true?—the same old faces behind the newspapers.

'Vengeance is mine. I will repay' is the motto of the book. Unlike its predecessor *War and Peace*, *Anna Karenina* is a fully adult work. Its themes are those of sexual love and death, and, too, that actions have consequences which we can no longer, as when young, lightly leave behind. Later our acts become our lives. We are to blame but we are not to blame. It is this new restraint, a new complexity, that sets the second book above the first.

The motto, the threat itself is an impersonal one. As such it is far more terrible, more effective than Tolstoy himself could be, reading the riot act to us. Similarly we see him incognito, sliding out of sight behind his characters. It is this latter aspect, tone and style, that in the last resort distinguishes the book. We are to blame and we are not to blame. We see this. We see it clearly; we see that the matter is complex. We understand that we cannot, dare not judge. But how, we ask, does the moralist, the author of *War and Peace*, come to bury the hatchet in this way?

In *Tolstoy and the Novel*, Mr John Bayley speaks of the fruitful tension set up in Tolstoy by the two sides of his nature—moralist and artist. The notion of some such tension, some division seeking resolution in art, is an accepted one. Yet in Tolstoy's case, where the division is at its most painful, it is possible never to think of this, so conditioned are we to view it as destructive. It is the moralist who wins the day. So that Mr Bayley's simple observation has the effect of something new and striking, of shedding a sudden illuminating light on the mystery. If the force of his appetite for life created Tolstoy the puritan, so too, to an extent, the moralist may be said to have served as anvil, to provide the ground, the battle-field on which Tolstoy fought to wrest artistic truth from moral truth.

The play, in *Anna Karenina*, is a reciprocal one. But how was it that this did occur to us? Tolstoy sweeps us away as the snowstorm in the darkness threatens to sweep Anna off her feet, when, alighting from the train which is taking her back to Moscow, she encounters Vronsky on the platform. The book has all the intensity of fantasy, of poetry. In this it may be said to have more in common with *Wuthering Heights* than with *War and Peace*. The conjunction is not itself unilluminating. To point the likeness is also, at once, to point the difference. For if in *Wuthering Heights* the passion rages with even greater intensity, the passion of Emily Brontë is, compared with Tolstoy's, virginal.

The book's very impact, our emotional involvement, its reality are curiously blinding. The strangest notions are to be found entrenched in the minds of its readers. There is, for example, the popular belief that if the critics' complaint in the case of *War and Peace* was that it neglected social problems, we have in *Anna Karenina* an indictment of society. To see the book as attacking the divorce laws, championing the cause of women's rights,

ANNA KARENINA

is a common error in flagrant contradiction of Tolstoy's views, an error that itself shows the need to look more closely. Divorce would scarcely solve Dolly's problems; it would not help Stepan Arkadyevitch (crippled by alimony he would be quite shorn of his carefree charm); early drafts of the novel in which Anna marries Vronsky still end with Anna's suicide. Sexual love is itself—here too—destructive and degrading; nor can marriage make a man happy.

To an extent, then, we may discount the anomaly, the gulf that seemed at first to yawn between the author of *War and Peace* and of *Anna*. But Anna dressed for the ball at which she dazzles Vronsky and cuts out Kitty, appears before us no less décolletée than Hélène. Despite this she has Tolstoy's sympathy. Yes, we have come a long way from Hélène, and from Natasha. There is much of Tolstoy himself in Anna. We feel that he recognises Anna's predicament, that he knows her, from experience, to be helpless.

There exist countless drafts of *Anna Karenina*.[1] In the first draft Anna is a vampire. The Karenins are called Stavrogitch. Professor Christian suggests that this may be an echo of Stavrogin, the name of Dostoevsky's devilish hero in *The Possessed*, the end of which had recently been published. There may be, he posits, a legacy from this early version in Kitty's observation at the ball, when, meeting her despairing gaze, Anna turns away and gaily begins talking to a neighbour: ' "Yes, there is some-

[1] See *Tolstoy: A Critical Introduction*, by R. F. Christian, Cambridge University Press.

thing uncanny, devilish and fascinating in her. . . ." ' The
early Karenin is a shy pedant, dreamy and eccentric. He
condones the liaison. Vronsky too is intelligent, high-
minded, sincerely in love with Kitty. Both men are
victimised by Anna, stout and even ugly, but already,
from the outset, invested with the charms of a courtesan.

In 1870 Tolstoy mentioned to Sonya his project of
depicting a type of society woman, married and gone
astray. The problem, Tolstoy explained, would be to
make her pitiable, not guilty. This plan was not pursued.
Two years later Anna Pirogova, a woman, plain, un-
married and certainly not well-born, the mistress of a
neighbour of the Tolstoys, threw herself under a train.
Tolstoy himself attended the post-mortem and for a
while, it appears, the features of this Anna superseded his
earlier conception.

At the time, however, he seems to have had no thought
of writing on, or, indeed, connecting these episodes. All
his creative thinking was enlisted by a novel, entailing
vast research, on Peter the Great. The subject failed to
come alive, and, to Sonya's horror, Tolstoy applied himself to learning Greek. After this phase he wrote three
school readers. Returning to his researches and his notes,
endlessly detailed descriptions of customs and of cos-
tume, Tolstoy complained that his novel made no pro-
gress. One evening he picked up a book, Pushkin's
Byelkin's Tales: 'The guests arrived at the country-
house.' That was how novels should start. Then and
there, we are told, he seized his pen and wrote: 'After the
opera the guests re-assembled at the house of the young
Countess Vraski.' Later transposed, transmuted into

ANNA KARENINA

Part II, Chapter 6, such was the opening of *Anna Karenina*.

The book's obstinate struggle to assert its independence in the teeth of Tolstoy's original thesis is evidence of its subconscious or unconscious strength. The fact that Tolstoy's attention was elsewhere, diverted, wholly absorbed by his labours on Peter the Great, had the effect of leaving the fantasy free, not merely to germinate but to establish itself in, as it were, the monster's very jaws. Three years earlier Tolstoy had spoken of his idea for a novel on a woman in society who commits adultery; he had, in fact, gone on from this to speak of how no sooner had he conceived the woman herself than all the supporting characters grouped themselves around her. These characters based, as was his habit, on persons Tolstoy knew, had been left, their presence unsuspected, to develop away from their prototypes in a manner which was, indeed, scarcely one of which Tolstoy could approve. They resolutely refused to fit the mould prepared for them. Tolstoy himself refused to compromise. The book was constantly put aside. The author detested his work. The action on him of so much that was alien, the need to digest and make terms with this, were none the less salutary. Never again would Tolstoy be so honest, honest as only art can—as it is art's job to—make us. To the remoteness from his own ideas, was added, as I have said, the element of distance, of looking back on a world he had not quite left, but from which he divined he would soon be, like his heroine, an exile. Tolstoy was looking his last on the social world, on the scenes of his own youth, looking back, moreover, in the light of a bitter knowledge. Reading *Anna Karenina* one wonders whether Sonya had not already threatened suicide. We know that Tolstoy, like Levin, removed the rope from his room and ceased to carry a gun when he went out. Even the obsession with railway stations comes, in the light of his death, to seem like a premonition.

Levin himself is late arriving on the scene. Early drafts deal merely with Anna and Vronsky. With Levin, Tolstoy enters the book—a Tolstoy, however, without the reasons for Leo Tolstoy's own despair. This acedia is not, it is true, a disease confined to artists. A failure to find fulfilment in their living may none the less be seen as a frequent, if not integral, concomitant of most creative work. What is an artist to do when he is not working? Or rather what can he do that will satisfy him? No other occupation offers such full employment. Thus Vronsky, we note, deprived of his profession, instinctively turns to art as perhaps the only occupation open to an exile. Only the Kittys are happy, the Kittys and the peasants. Why? The answer seems to us quite simple. It does not occur either to Tolstoy or to Levin—that Kitty does not ask if she is happy, she does not pause to ask. Her eyes are turned elsewhere. All the same if Levin were unfaithful would not Kitty, like Dolly, complain that life is harsh, would not existence seem a desert to her? But Levin is not unfaithful. He, like Tolstoy himself, is happy in his wife and in his children. Tolstoy is unhappy because he is an artist, incapable of living in the moment. Charades, skating, riding, these are no solace to him. What he needs is hard manual labour. The great mowing scene in *Anna*

Karenina describes Levin's fear that he may collapse: 'He thought of nothing, wished for nothing' but 'not to be left behind'. Levin, we read, lost 'all count of time. . . . More and more often now came those moments of oblivion, when it was possible not to think of what one was doing. The scythe cut of itself. Those were happy moments.' Again we read, 'The longer Levin mowed the oftener he experienced those moments of oblivion when it was not his arms which swung the scythe but the scythe seemed to mow of itself . . . and as though by magic . . . the work did itself regularly and carefully. These', Tolstoy tells us, 'were the most blessed moments.' The theme, repeated, could scarcely be more explicit. Whether an invocation to living in the moment, or whether addressed to Morpheus, to oblivion, both are a blotting-out of the thought that we must die. This is the very function and virtue of pleasure, to absolve us from the tormenting sense that everything is pointless, from the incurable need to find a point. As Levin says: ' "You would hardly believe how good this kind of thing is for every sort of foolishness." '

By bringing in Levin, Tolstoy tethered the drama of Anna and Vronsky to his own life and preoccupations. He tethered it to reality. When after we have spent three months (three chapters) with Levin in the country, Stepan Arkadyevitch unexpectedly arrives to shoot, we own we feel relieved. Strung up as we are by Anna's plight it is hard to be left looking out on the muddy winter furrows. Levin can at times be ponderous. He is not the kind of person whom we meet in books. He has no sense of the appropriate moment—as is shown by his

rambling on after Anna's death, when, debating his faith
or lack of faith, he is distinctly mal à propos, inept as a
panacea. His wedding, the last minute loss of his bride-
groom's outfit, the ceremony itself, all treated with needless detail, all this we feel is far too inessential to have
been invented. (It is, in fact, Tolstoy's wedding.) *It is this
needless detail that makes it real.* Kitty herself is nothing if
not *terre à terre.* Without this second story, we may feel,
the other, the drama might take off and fly away in the
storm like Anna's little red bag into the darkness.

In fact, if the need for Levin arose, and indeed sur-
vived—Tolstoy's tormenting doubts and horror of death
were far too insistent not to be included in the book—his
function was not to act as a sheet anchor, but rather to
serve as a foil, to heighten not hobble the drama. The book
is sufficiently tethered in other ways, by its psychology
and by its architecture. The evidence of persons who read
Russian, and thus have access to Tolstoy's successive
early drafts, suggests that there is a process of calling
back, a gradual transmutation of Tolstoy's somewhat far-
fetched, original characters back into himself. Anna is
much like Sonya. Love does not prevent two people being
sealed off in separate boxes.

Levin may be like Tolstoy, but so too may Vronsky.
First conceived as a buccaneering type who wears a ring
in his ear (this is 'a family habit') Tolstoy transfers
Vronsky to high society. He is a man whom Tolstoy
knows through and through. When as a boy in the Corps
of Pages someone refuses Vronsky a loan, he determines
never again to place himself in this position. Later he is, in

fact, short of funds—he has given his half of his father's vast estate to his married brother. He does not, however, think of applying to the latter. He has refused an offer of advancement, an action which he assumes will appear disinterested. Its effect is to lead to his being passed over. There is a stoicism in Vronsky, however, that both gives him a dignity and allows him to enjoy life. Typically, after the races he does not give way to despair but gets up early and tackles his accounts. The task acts as a purgative—he is in excellent spirits. By this time (p. 336) Anna is pregnant and desperate. 'Vronsky's life', on the other hand, we read, 'was particularly happy in that he had a code . . . which defined with unfailing certitude what should and should not be done.' With how much savage delight Tolstoy sets himself to compile this code: One must pay card-sharpers but need not pay tailors, must never lie to a man but may to a woman, must never cheat but may cheat a husband, must never pardon an insult but may give one.

' "Good, splendid!" he said to himself, crossing his legs, and taking a leg in his hand felt the springy muscle of the calf where he had bruised it the day before in his fall [in the races]. . . . He enjoyed the slight ache in his strong leg, he enjoyed the muscular sensation of movement in his chest as he breathed: The bright, cold August day which had made Anna feel so hopeless seemed exhilarating to him. . . . Everything he saw through the carriage window was as fresh and jolly and vigorous as he was himself: the roofs of the houses shining in the setting sun, the sharp outlines of fences and angles of buildings, even the fields of potatoes—everything was beautiful like a lovely landscape fresh from the artist's brush and lately varnished.'

Never again, in fact, will Vronsky be so happy. He has without knowing it crossed the watershed; he crossed it at the moment in which Anna gave herself to him. The trap closed on him then with her words: ' "I have nothing but you left" ', words of which he does not see the import—they are the words of a woman who feels herself drowning and will not fail to drag him down with her. Already when Anna seems dying, at this early date, Vronsky's humiliation appears complete: 'He felt thrust out from the ordered way he had hitherto trodden so proudly and lightly.' We do well to remember Vronsky's pride and, too, his stoicism. Later these qualities will make him stern. Meanwhile ' "This is how people go mad", he said . . . "and shoot themselves, to escape humiliation", he added slowly.'

Recalling all this, we are taken aback by the tone Tolstoy adopts to Vronsky when we meet him abroad with Anna. So hostile is it we wonder if we have not misunderstood. We recall the irony of the 'code'. But Tolstoy can and does, we feel, write in this way because he in his youth subscribed to such a code. He hits at Vronsky but Vronsky is an aspect of himself, he is still flesh of Tolstoy's flesh. The tone Tolstoy now adopts is another matter. No doubt attacking Italy as the resort of those 'lovers of art' who, in reality, go there simply because it is fashionable to do so, he presents the lovers to us alone and together at last in an uncharacteristic, elaborate description of the palazzo they live in. 'The palazzo', we are mysteriously told, 'sustained Vronsky in the agreeable illusion that he was not so much a Russian landed proprietor' (a position he has never filled or indeed aspired to fill) or an 'equerry without a post, as an enlightened connoisseur and patron of the arts. . .' This we are told was 'the role chosen by Vronsky . . . he even took to wearing a hat and flinging his cloak over his shoulder in the medieval fashion—a style that was very becoming to him.'

All this is said in a new, unpleasant, sneering way which takes us back to the end of *War and Peace*. It reminds us of Tolstoy's unreasonable moods, of how unfair he could be to people he misjudged as insincere. The tone is not maintained, but for a moment hate shines out—for a moment Vronsky is alien, is no longer a retrospective aspect of Tolstoy himself. Or is this a side of himself which Tolstoy knows—the hate resembles self-hate—hate for the imitation peasant in his blouse who is Count Tolstoy?

This is the hate of the artist for the dilettante,[1] hatred for those who play at what is serious. The tone here is unbalanced, that of a man who knows this view of things is normally reversed. In the eyes of the world it is the artist who plays at life. Art is a relaxation for leisure hours. Tolstoy is on the defensive; he is also here as nowhere else in *Anna Karenina*, on the verge of attacking us, of reading us a lecture. Anger instead is conquered, laid aside, the diatribe transmuted into tragedy, into the remainder of the book—an indictment of those who, like Anna and Vronsky, play at life. Poor Vronsky! The attack seems hardly fair. He has never known a normal

[1] See *Anna Karenina and other Essays*, by F. R. Leavis, Chatto.

family or even country life. At a stroke he has lost profession, friends, light-hearted banter, the framework so
fundamental, essential to a man of his conventional stamp.
It is small wonder, surely, if he is disorientated. Later,
his attempts to make life real, to create a life for himself in
the country earn him our respect and sympathy no less
than they do Dolly's. It is true that the hospital, the tennis,
the elections are very different from Levin's country life.
We cannot picture Vronsky like Levin out at dawn putting up grouse and snipe with his dog, Lasca.

Descriptions of Vronsky's country life do not, in fact,
include any sense that we are in the country. Faced with
the following passage in an examination we would have
no trouble in placing it: 'The moon had lost all its lustre
and was like a white cloud in the sky. Not a single star
could be seen. The sedge, silvery before, now shone like
gold. The stagnant pools were all like amber. The blue of
the grass had changed to yellow-green. . . . A hawk woke
up and settled on a haycock, turning its head from side to
side and looking discontentedly at the marsh. Crows were
flying about the field and a bare-legged boy was driving
the horses to an old man who had got up from under his
coat and was combing his hair. The smoke from the gun
was white as milk over the green of the grass. . . .'[1]

We are not told that Levin notices these things. That
he does so is none the less implied. Through them we
become Levin, we partake of his being, his mood born
of the morning, his successful shoot, of his being out
there alone and witnessing these events which the others,
still asleep, are missing. We are ourselves as exalted as if

[1] Constance Garnett's translation.

we too had been out and seen the day breaking in the fields.

This is not Vronsky's happiness. We are in no danger of mistaking the context of this passage. And yet what is noted is purely factual—it could be Richard Jeffreys. Tolstoy, we feel, is back from an early walk. Taking his diary he jots down: 'Pools amber-coloured. Blue of the grass changing to yellow-green. Hawk turning its head from side to side on a haycock. . . .' These are the keen-eyed notes of the countryman. There is no attempt to *use* these phenomena, to make of them a second thing with words: 'The smoke of my gun as white as milk against the green grass.' This is an image born of the thing seen. If the note has—and it has here—a poetic felicity, the poetry is, in fact, sheer accuracy. Tolstoy, we may be certain, noted it on the spot. Condemned as he was by his stature to solitude, we may feel that he found his greatest pleasure in nature, the only sensual pleasure that was guiltless. In nature too he found a distraction from himself. If Levin's pleasure in the early morning rests upon, is underpinned by his happiness with Kitty, he is affected, changed by what he sees. Levin's is not a monologue but a dialogue with nature. Whereas Vronsky's view from the carriage window is a wholly subjective one. Significantly what he sees is houses. It is a built-up landscape which he contemplates. Vronsky is essentially a townsman.

Meeting him we feel that Vronsky is a man who has never known unhappiness. His expression is good-humoured, calm and resolute. He remains imperturbably at ease, unruffled by Levin's apparently irrational irritation. This early confrontation of Vronsky and Levin, who after this rarely encounter one another in the flesh, allows Tolstoy to state his opposing themes. We do not see the two men as polar opposites. Vronsky like Levin is open and unaffected. In other circumstances we feel Levin would have liked him. Later, Anna herself meeting Levin, sees their similarity and understands why Kitty should have been in love with these two men.

The contrast between the two is none the less fundamental. It is at once so deep, so inconspicuous that if we note their situations as foils to one another we may not think of contrasting the couples themselves. Kitty is not in Anna's class. The two stories, moreover, are set in such totally different keys that it is hard to connect them; we go from one world to another. It is like hanging a Rembrandt by a Corot.

It is in fact not without interest to turn back and look up the chapter in which we have our first sight of Vronsky. As we recall it he made a poor impression on us. He was very much the conventional hero. This, we told ourselves, is Tolstoy 'doing a Ouida'. Vronsky only assumes interest for us, emerges from the unremarkable ranks to which he belongs, by chance—the chance that makes him Anna's lover.

This is wholly incorrect. Recalling the common delusion that the book is about women's rights, we may wonder if any book was ever, at all points, so oddly subject to misinterpretation. Never was any love less due to accident. Anna and Vronsky are born to meet, to love. They are made for one another. As to the first impression he made on us, we see, if we look up this chapter, that we were prejudiced, that we looked at Vronsky through Levin's eyes. Or rather we were unfair to Vronsky, since we preferred Levin with whom we were emotionally involved.

We may recall Tolstoy's words apropos of *Anna*: no sooner had he thought of this type of woman than all the other characters grouped themselves around her. In his autobiography Julian Green describes his own discovery that he could not think of plots—he was not the least interested in plots. Despairing, ill at ease in his hotel bedroom, he reflects that the seeds of his first novel had been not a plot but a place, a room in his own home. He thinks now of the chocolate-coloured drawing-room, with its rows of somewhat funereal family photographs. What would he not give to be there now! And suddenly he is! He is someone—who?—a woman standing in front of those photographs: who is she? But someone calls; someone, another woman, is calling to her from another room. And all at once he is off, writing *Adrienne Mesurat*. So it is with Tolstoy's characters. 'The fault, dear Brutus, lies not in our stars, but in ourselves. . . .' Cassius's remark is a tautology. For we are foredoomed, as by the stars, by what is in ourselves. To an extent what happens does not lie within our power to control any more than it lies in our power to change our gifts or limitations. The strength, the peculiar force of *Anna Karenina* consists in this, its psychological truth. Actions, events are simply the logical, natural outcome of the fact that these people are as they are.

I have spoken of its peculiar force, of its fatality.

During, for Tolstoy, the trying period between *War and Peace* and *Anna Karenina*, he suddenly decided to learn Greek. 'Within a few weeks,' says M. Troyat, 'he had outdistanced his teacher.... As he tramped through the snow ... up to his calves, his head was filled with sun, marble and geometry.' It was also filled with the new aspiration, noted down by Sonya 'to write something pure and elegant, from which not one word could be removed, like the works of Greek literature and art'. As he read Homer his head was surely filled with something more than a new ideal of classical perfection—with a new concept of man's tragic stature, with something Tolstoy recognised: men the force of whose passions led them to externalise these as Gods. The Greek world was not all geometry, all symposiums. It was also a sea-girt, sea-faring race of adventurers forged by the elements, by the wine-dark sea. It was man, too, at the mercy of himself, the pawn of the quarrelsome gods, of Aphrodite, Athene, the victim of Olympian domestic strife. It was not only the agora but the murkier, blood-stained stage of Mycenae, of the Agamemnon.

I find it hard to accept M. Troyat's verdict that Tolstoy's learning Greek had no effect on the writing of *Anna Karenina*. It seems to me, on the contrary, fundamental. This and this only explains the new dramatic note, the intensity of *Anna Karenina*, an intensity markedly absent from his earlier work, where indeed the effect is gained precisely by a debunking of drama, a cult of simplicity, by a disarming childlike ingenuousness.

The note of *Anna Karenina* is, rather, elemental. Anna's and Vronsky's love is like the snow-storm. It rages despite themselves. It is, as it were, inhuman and destructive. Anna and Vronsky are caught in a web represented for us by a web of recurring images. Their story is like a nightmare from which there is no escape. Everything in it has a significance. The colour even, the red, of Anna's little bag; we sense it coming towards us in the darkness as the snow whirls around us and we hear the hiss of steam; figures loom up, dim shapes on the platform; below on the rails the light of a lantern illumines a man crouching, hammering, doing something to the couplings. This is the muttering gnome-like figure of Anna's and Vronsky's nightmares. The lantern prefigures Anna's guttering candle. Already on p. 8 we meet the Oblonsky children playing trains outside their father's study:

'They were dragging something along and had upset it.

' "I told you not to sit passengers on the roof," cried the little girl in English, "Now, pick them up!" '

The railway, a new rapid mode of travel, is itself symbolic of the relentless force bearing Anna and Vronsky to destruction.

Vronsky is predestined to love a married woman. He has never cared for young girls, and has always, hitherto, sought his pleasure with the 'Claras'. Not only have he and Anna much in common; they have that slightly incestuous resemblance to one another which so often characterises lovers. Thus Vronsky's expression and Anna's step are both 'resolute'. Both have lacked a normal family background. To Vronsky husbands are slightly absurd; he prefers bachelor life. Dolly finds Anna's house unhomely. Both Anna and Vronsky are carefree; they have nothing to be ashamed of and are consequently off their guard. At the same time both frequent Petersburg society; both have drunk the dangerous elixir, imbibed, without being conscious of doing so, the tone of a faster set than the note of more provincial Moscow.

That which brings them together serves also to divide them. Thus, pride in both engenders humiliation, which, in its turn, engenders feelings of resentment. Each blames the other for his sufferings. That which first attracted Vronsky in Anna now repels him. He no longer desires a mistress figure. Physical love will not suffice to fill the empty hours. Vronsky yearns for wife, home, children. Anna's very charms have a cloying effect on him. Love becomes a form of imprisonment, an element from which he longs only to escape. That same society which once threw them together now divides them, since Vronsky is received but Anna not. Even when Vronsky is happiest in the country, the lack in both him and Anna of any inner reserves makes their life peculiarly artificial. They live in the country as if in a luxury hotel. Vronsky is not only tied to Anna; he is restricted in other ways, by his limitations. He cannot, like Levin, spend the night on a haycock. He is not free to do so. He is not, that is to say, mentally free, as Levin is, to muse. Levin is an eccentric. Vronsky is conventional. It is this which gives him his tragic stature.

It is also this which earns him our respect. Engulfed no less than Anna by their hate, Vronsky reminds us of some trapped savage beast at bay—he none the less retains a dignity, possible only, perhaps, to those sustained by a 'code'. True he has long 'felt thrust from the ordered way along which he had hitherto trodden so proudly and lightly'. Nevertheless Vronsky does not rat. (Levin, I feel, with all his integrity, would have deserted Anna, just as he longed to flee from his brother's death-bed.)

Whereas love diminished him, hate exalts Vronsky. Admittedly his love is not, like Anna's, infected by the further degrading emotion—jealousy. Vronsky hates in resistance to degradation. His hate is the healthy hate of the good animal he is. In place of his smile showing 'his strong white teeth', we see the cruel menacing look in his eyes that Anna dreads. Vronsky does not go under as Anna does. It lies, however, with Anna to deal the final mortal blow. Her intention is to make him suffer. In this she is so successful that at our last encounter with him we can scarcely recognise him. Can this really be Count Vronsky, the famous lover, pacing the platform with Stepan Arkadyevitch? It is as if we have read and thought so much about him that, as so often, reality disappoints. It would no longer occur to us to think of this man as handsome. His face, aged and suffering, looks stony. He is wearing a long overcoat. This coat, a military greatcoat, is his sole surviving romantic attribute. He raises his hat abstractedly. The parting is oddly painless—Vronsky, unheroically, has toothache. The moment has no significance. For him, no less than for us, his exit is a mere postscript to the drama.

The fact that it is left to Vronsky's mother to tell us, to compress into a single sentence, the tale of Vronsky's sufferings after Anna's death, their terror that he would do away with himself, minimises the effect of this revelation. If he was once a typical military man, a man, that is, of a limited unimaginative cast of mind, passion—love and hate—have changed all this. He is never unaware of Anna's sufferings, nor does he remain indifferent to them. He is not insensitive but merely helpless, powerless in the face of her irrationality.

Limited he may once have been. He is no longer so. Even at our final meeting with him, he is not, as we supposed, incapable of feeling. Walking now on the platform with Levin's brother, he is suddenly overcome by the sight of the rails, the tender. The terrible memories all come crowding back—Anna's revenge, the mangled body in the waiting-room, 'that fearful threat—that he would be sorry for it'. He tries to recall their best moments together, but these, even, are poisoned. For a second he is beside himself. Then regaining control he calmly mentions the battle. ' "You've not seen any dispatch since yesterday's? ..." ' A decisive engagement, he says, is expected for the morrow. 'And after a few words about the proclamation of Milan as King ... they returned to their respective carriages at the ringing of the second bell.'

Reading this sentence we do not realise that this is our parting with Vronsky. The book continues for some twenty pages, still further effacing an exit which is as unobtrusive as his first appearance on the stage.

The contrast between Vronsky's unrhetorical withdrawal and Anna's exit are worth pondering. It illustrates not the likeness but the gulf between the lovers. Why did Vronsky fall in love with Anna? We have said that he was predestined to love a married woman. But then why not a Liza Merkalova? There are plenty of such women in Princess Betsy's set. Indeed it is entirely composed of them.

But Vronsky shunned the drawing-rooms. He preferred the Claras. This is as much as to say he dislikes the
Lizas. We recall his mother's history, his ambiguous
relation to her. We recall, too, Princess Betsy's set with
its petty, malicious gossip. Significantly the men are background figures. The lovers are barely distinguishable from
the betrayed husbands reduced to carrying their wives'
shawls. But Vronsky is no lap-dog. We recall his pride.
Disposed of early in the Corps of Pages, left to fend for
himself, without love or family, Vronsky's sole possession
is his honour. And suddenly we see that Vronsky is not,
after all, deficient in potential as a hero. This is no mere
socialite. We see that to fall in love Vronsky needed a
woman such as Anna, a woman above suspicion, of unim-
peachable virtue, a woman whose conquest will be worthy
of him. We see that the fates are inexorable; or, to put it
another way, that Tolstoy's psychology is indeed relentless.

' "Anna and transgression,"[1] says Dolly, "I cannot
connect the two." ' And it is true that illicit love, the
shame, the petty deceptions are utterly foreign to Anna,
so much so that they permanently unhinge her.

What then exactly is meant by the not uncommon view
that Stepan Arkadyevitch paves the way for Anna, that
his function is to give us an insight into Anna that we
might not otherwise possess?[2] This is not far removed
from the popular conviction that what Tolstoy is seeking

[1] ' "Anna and sin", says Dolly, "I cannot connect the two." '
Constance Garnett's translation seems to me happier.

[2] Mr John Bayley (*Tolstoy and the Novel*, Chatto and Windus,
p. 213) sees him 'as a kind of index to her'; and (p. 205) writes: 'It
is through him that we first perceive and understand her.'

to demonstrate is that a man gets away with it where a woman cannot. In fact the book is filled with immoral women; that is, with married women in the highest circles blithely engaged in a series of liaisons, who lead, in short, exactly the life of a Stepan Arkadyevitch. When, after Anna has fallen in love with Vronsky, she forces herself, as a punishment, to confess to Dolly the reason why she is leaving Moscow early, this is in pointed contrast to her brother whose own practice has been—this is Dolly's complaint—to tell her nothing. At one point, it is true, in the course of their conversation Anna does appear to echo Stiva: ' "But truly . . . I am not to blame, or only a little bit," she said . . . drawling the words "a little bit". "Oh how like Stiva you said that", ' Dolly exclaims laughing. Anna is hurt. ' "Oh no . . . I am not Stiva." ' No sooner has she indignantly refuted the idea ' . . . "that I could let myself doubt myself for an instant," ' than she feels this is untrue. She does, in fact, doubt herself. But, unlike Stiva, she is going away.

She doubts herself—as we may all have cause to doubt ourselves. Let us not forget that she has lived unscathed for eight years in Petersburg, a city of loose morals, where scandal is the very breath of life.

Her confidence in herself is, in fact, her Achilles heel. In all this she is quite unlike her brother. Not only is Stepan Arkadyevitch far from virtuous. Nothing that can conceivably befall him will raise him to the ranks of a tragic figure. If Anna is asked what she is thinking of her answer is invariably: ' "Of the same thing" ' (of Vronsky, of their love, of the divorce), whereas her brother cannot even remember his marital crisis. He is forever forgetting and remembering. Despite his plight he cannot repress a sense of his own well-being; he cannot help enjoying life as usual. As for the woman in the case: ' "And the worst of it is that she is now . . . Everything happens just to spite me! Oh dear, what am I to do?" ' The answer is: forget oneself and the luckless governess, who is far from evoking a grand passion.

Stepan Arkadyevitch is Offenbach, *opéra bouffe*. In what way can he throw light on Anna? What exactly is meant by this—that there is a weak strain, a depravity in the blood of the Oblonskys that has yet to show itself, to make its appearance in Anna? This does not seem particularly helpful. It implies an unpleasantly moral tone. Few of us are tried as Anna is. At most it endows her, surely, with a buoyant disposition, a temperament that carries her cheerfully through her marriage with Karenin. But even this itself can be explained by the fact that, brought up by an aunt, she, a penniless orphan, was lucky enough to secure Karenin. She carries herself erect; with her light rapid step this constitutes her peculiar distinction. Her handshake, too, is characteristic—frank and energetic. Does her carriage suggest a need, a habit of bracing herself or is it that she has never had cause to stoop, that she has no shameful recollections? This would make her subsequent degradation the more painful. Her conscience hitherto has made her happy, the consciousness of successfully filling her role as Karenin's wife, a man twenty years older than herself and calculated to inspire at least a certain fear, certain doubts in a girl from the provinces. We remind ourselves that she is now a Petersburg *grande dame*, that Dolly is a little afraid of her.

A DARING COIFFEUR

For the question we ask about Anna, that at once comes
to mind, is: What is the cause of her animation? How,
married to Karenin, is her step so light, how can she be so
vividly alive? Partly, no doubt, it is that she shares her
brother's nature, his naturally sweet, sanguine disposition—because, if you will, she is a woman made for love,
made, that is, to respond to life, made for something for
which she is, without knowing it, still waiting. . . .

But surely contrast far exceeds resemblance. Is not the
point, the whole point, about Stepan Arkadyevitch that he
is born to be unfaithful? Men are made like this, as Dolly
herself reasons, staying with Anna and Vronsky in the
country. If Anna seeks to hold Vronsky by her looks, her
charms, great as these are, she will fail to hold him. The
first of her husband's mistresses, Dolly bitterly muses, did
not keep him by her attractiveness. Had Stiva, in fact, been
a woman, he would have been no less inconstant, as fickle,
as lightly forgiven by society, as that same charming
childlike Liza Merkalova whose position Anna finds so
puzzling.

' "But do tell me, I never could make it out," began
Anna after a pause, speaking in a tone that showed she
was not putting an idle question . . . "do tell me— what
are her relations with Prince Kaluzhky, Mishka, as they
call him? I come across them very little. What exactly is
their relation?" Betsy's eyes twinkled, and she looked
keenly at Anna. It is, she explains, a new fashion. "They've
all adopted it. They have kicked over the traces. But there
are ways and ways of doing it." '

The role of Stepan Arkadyevitch is to sound the theme,

as in an overture, to introduce it; to play as a child might play with something the appalling significance of which he has no inkling.

We catch the theme at the outset. The tone is serio-comic, mingling with that of Levin's love affair. Again, as if by chance, it is there to greet Vronsky on his return to his rooms in Petersburg. Petritsky's mistress installed, resplendent in lilac satin, filling the room with her Parisian chatter, complains of her husband's refusal to grant her a divorce. ' "Do you understand the folly of it? That on the pretext of my being unfaithful to him . . . he wants to get the benefit of my fortune." ' [1] The irony reaches its climax in Vronsky's laughing tale of being sent to pacify an outraged husband.

Anna herself comes to Moscow bound on a similar mission, to reconcile her brother and his wife. How blooming she looks, as poor Dolly enviously observes: ' "I? Yes," ' says Anna absently, in the careless tone of one who takes such things for granted. It is she who calms Dolly's jealousy, who actually trots out the cliché that men despise such women, that the home is always sacred to them.

The theme, the melody is indeed a mocking one. In the end the wheel comes full circle. The roles are reversed. It is Anna's turn now to be unhappy, Anna now, who, ravaged by jealousy, appears before us reduced to a still more lethal form of Dolly's helpless, indecisive state.

Meanwhile we are still puzzled. What is the explanation, the secret of Anna's singular radiance? It is morning, day-light, when we first meet her. Despite this, we have the

[1] Translation, Constance Garnett.

sense that the blinds are drawn, the lights still on in the railway carriage into which Vronsky mounts. Standing aside at the door of the compartment, Vronsky, we feel, is in shadow—a figure in a greatcoat. As he turns to look at her again, Anna too looks round. Divining from his mother's talk in the carriage who Vronsky is, 'her brilliant grey eyes, shadowed by thick lashes, gave him a friendly, attentive look', before turning away. In that look 'Vronsky had time to notice the suppressed animation which played over her face. . . . It was as though her nature were so brimming over with something, that against her will it expressed itself now in a radiant look, now in a smile. . . .'

Later we are told 'that every time they met her heart quickened with the same feeling that had seized her in the train the day she first saw him'. Partly then Anna's radiance on this occasion is already, from the outset, attributable to Vronsky. It is also due to Seriozha, the son on whom she has lavished all her store of love, the fullness of love she could not give Karenin, a love which has, in fact, kept her alive. Looking back on it, we detect the omen, the fatal early conjunction of Vronsky and Seriozha. Anna and Countess Vronsky, Vronsky's mother, have passed the night exchanging stories about their sons. Afterwards Anna actually exchanges Seriozha for Vronsky. In her first flush of happiness she forgets her son. Later, restless and ostracised in Moscow, she blames Vronsky for parting her from Seriozha. Her strange failure to love Vronsky's child is due both to the fact that Vronsky is all she needs and that Annie is not Seriozha.

Meanwhile, in Petersburg, her life is centred on him.

Dolly has been to see her in Petersburg, but Anna has never been to see the Oblonskys in Moscow. This unusual break in her routine is itself exhilarating. She has laid aside her maternal role. Travel, moreover, serves to relieve us of our ties. Added to this, she is going to see her brother, her sole blood relation and a dreadful scapegrace, who is himself as good as a holiday. One does not need to be Anna, married to Karenin, to divine the pleasure she feels on seeing him, to be a Vronsky to note the naturalness, lack of constraint, that characterises her relations with him. Without being aware of it, Anna is already déracinée, breathing in a simpler, freer air.

The provincial, less sophisticated atmosphere of Moscow has the effect of throwing her off her guard. It allows her to set off home with an untroubled conscience. ' "Well, that's all over and thank heaven," ' she thinks, as the third bell rings and she takes her seat in the train. ' "Tomorrow I will see Seriozha, Alexei Alexandrovitch, and my life—my nice everyday life—will go on as before." ' She has no regrets.

Even when she encounters Vronsky on the platform and hears from him the words she longs to hear, she replies as she ought to have replied. No, she has nothing to blush for. Once when she confided to her husband that one of his subordinates had paid her marked attention, Karenin had dismissed the incident. All women in society were liable to such things. There can be no question of confessions.

Despite this, she forms the habit of going where Vronsky goes and everywhere he speaks to her of love. She does not face her feelings until, on one occasion,

Vronsky fails to come as she expected. The disappointment she feels finally opens her eyes. At this she does not
hesitate to act. She roundly tasks Vronsky with his
behaviour to Kitty and forbids him to utter the word love
to her: ' "I have never had to blush in front of anyone
before but you make me feel as if I were guilty of something." ' The sole result of this conversation is that
Vronsky's replies serve to inflame Anna more than ever.
The prolonged tête-à-tête does not escape unnoticed.
Karenin, who is present, observing this but still trusting
his wife, resolves to caution her. He sits up waiting for
her in her boudoir.

Karenin's treatment at Tolstoy's hands seems to me no
less unfair than the dislike he engenders in his readers.
This does not mean that one may not, in life, intensely
dislike such persons. One may feel them as against life.
In Tolstoy, however, the harshness with which he allows
himself to treat Karenin seems to me unworthy. It is also
confusing. Critics are for the most part in agreement that
our picture of Anna's marriage is itself unclear. On her
return Anna is looking forward not only to seeing
Seriozha but to seeing her husband, to 'her nice everyday
life'. Even if this is merely the desire for security, it does
not imply that her marriage is unhappy. That it is not
unhappy is confirmed in other ways: just as she is for a
moment disappointed in Seriozha—'she had pictured him
nicer than he . . . was'—so she notices her husband's ears.

In other words she has never noticed before that his
ears stick out, they have never before offended her.
Indeed, on the very same evening of her return from

Moscow, she accompanies her husband to his study; slipping her arm through his she inquires what he is reading. He likes to read theology, politics. He is wholly lacking in any feeling for the arts; despite this he makes a point of 'keeping up', of reading about such things in order to talk about them, or so Tolstoy witheringly informs us. At present, he says, he is reading *Poésie des Enfers*. It is as if he said he were reading Rimbaud. We cannot repress a smile. Anna too smiles. And how, we may inquire, does Anna smile? Tolstoy is explicit: Anna smiles at her husband 'as people smile at the foibles of those they love'.

Added to this we learn that Anna has, in fact, lived in a very close relation to her husband, that if he went to bed five minutes later than usual she noticed it and asked the reason why. Nor is this all. As Karenin himself recalls, with pain, Anna has always confided everything to him. ' . . . she always immediately told him all her joys, pleasures and sorrows.' Now when he attempts to caution Anna, 'He saw that the depths of her soul, always before open to him, were now closed against him . . . she seemed to be saying straight out to him: "Yes, my heart is closed and so it should be and will be in future." Now he felt like a man who returns home to find his own house locked against him. "But perhaps the key may yet be found," thought Karenin.'

We are already acquainted with the sarcastic tone it is Karenin's habit to adopt, as when he comes to meet his wife at the station. The fact that, in the midst of his many duties, he comes at all, suggests this tone might be designed to hide his feelings. This being so, it comes to seem less strange that Anna should entertain so little fear of him, should have opened her heart to him as she has done.

A coherent thread may be traced. It is, however, extracted from a mass of contradictory material. Or rather it is extracted not so much from the facts as from the way they are presented to us. The facts, if we subject them to careful scrutiny, do not provide the indictment we expect. For, for some reason, we have conceived a dislike for him from the start. But—all of us are unlikeable! It offends us that Tolstoy should extend the tolerance he does to all his main characters but Karenin. No doubt it is indispensable to the structure of the story that Anna should have a husband of this type. But to be born Karenin is itself a tragedy. In making a butt of him in this way Tolstoy obscures what might be clear and sinks to the cheap device of making him the villain of the piece.

We dislike him from the moment when we first set eyes on him, because of his hat, because his ears stick out, because he is Anna's husband, and, as such, is in the way. Attired for bed, in pyjamas and dressing-gown, the thought that as Anna's husband he has conjugal rights sends a chill of horror down our spine.

Our view of him is dictated by our feeling for Anna and Vronsky. It rests on a very slight acquaintance with him, dating from long before we see him at close quarters, waiting up for Anna in her boudoir.

He is waiting to caution Anna not because he is jealous but because she has given cause for gossip. Jealousy itself he regards as a shameful emotion. We would be inclined to agree with him. To Tolstoy this is a part of Karenin's opting out. Tolstoy's tone is queer to say the least. He is depicting a man into whose head there now enters the terrible thought that his wife may be unfaithful. Karenin, we are smoothly told, is 'face to face with life', that is 'with the possibility of his wife's loving someone other than himself, and this seemed to him very irrational and incomprehensible'—we are told, 'because it was life itself'.

' "The question," Karenin says, "of her feelings, is not my affair, but the affair of her conscience." ' Well, again we agree. It shows a respect for Anna. It shows, we may feel, a laudable restraint, as does the cold manner into which he falls confronted by Anna's intractable attitude. He does not behave badly. He behaves with dignity. But that is not what we are meant to feel. And indeed, this is my point, the reader does not feel it. He gladly swallows what Tolstoy feeds to him. It is, in fact, worth quoting the remainder of this passage: Alexei Alexandrovitch, we learn, had 'all his life . . . lived and worked in official spheres having to do with the reflection of life. And every time he had come up against life itself he had stepped aside. Now he experienced a sensation such as a man might feel who quietly crossing a bridge over a chasm, suddenly discovers that the bridge is broken and that the abyss yawns below. The abyss was real life; the bridge, that artificial existence Karenin had been leading. For the first time the possibility of his wife's falling in love with any-body occurred to him, and he was horrified.'

Karenin is depicted as denying life. And yet his be-haviour at this point seems very natural. He is not self-righteous. He is quite simply shattered. Karenin is a mutilated man. He is not bloodless; quite otherwise, he cannot bear women to weep because he himself finds this too upsetting.

If we trace it carefully his development has a logic. He does become dried up and inhuman. Suffering makes him so. This is scarcely surprising. His position has indeed been intolerable. Despite this, he does not think of casting Anna off, but hopes that with 'kindness, tenderness, persuasion' (strange words for Karenin, surely) Anna may come to her senses. When Anna tells him she is Vronsky's mistress one of his first feelings is of physical compassion. This is followed by immense relief. He experiences the sensation of a man who has had a tooth out, who after a long bout of toothache and the excruciating agony of the actual extraction, suddenly feels himself a new man.

Even after this and his repudiation of Anna, he is still capable of feeling, prepared to admit his feelings, and to love Anna's baby. He will do anything, anything Anna wants. It is small wonder, surely, if in the end he becomes vindictive. But somehow the logic is strangely lost on us.

We have hated him from the start, felt that he was obnoxious, that it was natural for Anna to take a lover. The facts may be against us—we admit them reluctantly. Why do we dislike him so intensely? Well, what about his ingratiating attitude to his superiors? Yes, we admit this is distasteful. But then his desire for power is a form of compensation. Tolstoy could have depicted it differently, could, more fairly, have mocked it as he at times mocks Levin. But no, in Karenin's case he is pitiless. Tolstoy cannot abide the man. Infusing us at the start with his dislike, the effect is to obscure our sense of Karenin's unfolding, with the result that much is far from clear.

Thinking back to the scene in the boudoir we recall its
oddness: for the first time the possibility of Anna's falling
in love with someone else—Vronsky?—occurs to him and
he is 'horrified'.

How many of us would not react in a similar way?
However firm the ground on which we tread, we too
would have exactly that sense of the crumbling bridge and
the chasm. Tolstoy's sneer here seems in doubtful taste.
The bridge we are told is Karenin's 'artificial existence';
the chasm which yawns below is 'life itself'. It is also—
can Tolstoy for a moment have forgotten?—the abyss
where Anna and Vronsky dwell.

Karenin's treatment at Tolstoy's hands seems to me a
weakness. Tolstoy does not himself become Karenin, nor,
as a result, do we, as we ourselves become in turn Anna,
Vronsky, Levin, Kitty. In this sense Karenin seems to me
unjustly represented. Had we been able to look out
through his eyes, the book must surely have gained in
depth. Moreover, as the husband in the case, it seems
peculiarly odd that he should not have a fair hearing. In
this do we not catch Tolstoy himself adhering to Vronsky's
bachelor view of husbands as slightly absurd? What, after
all, has Anna to recommend her? She is vain, idle, selfish,
irrational, uncontrolled. Her incredible egocentricity
passes unnoticed when, for example, taking leave of
Vronsky, she says she must go or she will be late for the
races. She entirely forgets it seems that Vronsky is riding
in them, and quite omits, it appears, to wish him luck.

With all her faults, then, Tolstoy contrives to inhabit
an Anna, to make us enter so fully into her being that we
neglect to judge her, so absorbed are we by her plight, so

wholly engulfed by her feelings that we fail to notice both his heroine's vices and Tolstoy's art. The book, as I have said, is compulsive reading and it is largely Anna who makes it so. In her we do not have *opéra bouffe*, not light but grand opera, violent passion, tragic arias. The book rightly bears her name—Anna dominates it, possessed, obsessed by her unhappiness. Everything about her is dramatic, tragic in contrast to the humdrum Oblonsky milieu. Yes, from her first appearance we feel it perfectly right that she should step to the centre of the stage. Thus Anna, as does Vronsky, imposes herself on nature. Even the trees give her back herself, serve merely to reflect, to confirm her unhappiness. Her attempts to dominate Vronsky, however, to deprive him of any function but to say: 'I love you', are the rock on which their love founders.

Professor Henri Troyat, who has the advantage of access to the still untranslated early drafts, contends that lover and husband are divested of their virtues, demoted in inverse proportion to Anna's rise.[1] That is, he says, they are demoted to exalt Anna. Tolstoy fell in love with his heroine. In other words Tolstoy is jealous of both Vronsky and Karenin. Possibly there is some truth in this. But there is also, at every turn, consummate artistry. Thus husband and lover are both named Alexei; this is embodied in Anna's nightmare where both make love to her. Anna is closely linked to the world of dreams. She comes to us from the shadowy world of fantasy, of the unconscious. The madness of her last fateful journey is already pre-figured, the way for that madness paved early on by her

[1] *Tolstoy*, by Henri Troyat, W. H. Allen.

overnight journey back from Moscow: seated in the compartment she cannot tell whether the train is going backwards or forwards or has come to a standstill. Is that Annushka sitting there beside her or a stranger? ' "What is that . . . a . . . cloak or an animal? And what am I doing here? Am I myself or someone else?" ' She is terrified by her own reflections. Just then the stoker, a peasant in a long-waisted nankeen coat, enters the carriage to check the thermometer. After this 'everything became confused again'; the peasant is gnawing something on the wall; 'the old woman stretched her legs the whole length of the carriage which she filled with a dark cloud; after that there was a terrible screech and clatter, as though someone were being torn to pieces; then a red light blinded her eyes, and at last a wall rose up and blotted everything out. Anna felt as if she were falling from a height. But . . . far from seeming dreadful' this 'was . . . pleasant'. She wakes to find someone—the guard—shouting in her ear and realises that they must have reached a station.

Not only do we see Anna behaving irrationally. She herself stands for the irrational. When we first meet her she is warm, impulsive—as such the obvious vehicle for passion. That Anna plays the part she does, does not, in my view, spring from Tolstoy's own infatuation with her, but rather, on the contrary, from his recognition of the role of passion in our lives. The irrational, Tolstoy is saying, dominates our vision; it is powerful; it is to be feared.

And yet we feel it is true that Tolstoy does like Anna *because* she is capable of passion. She is open, unafraid, she does not, like Karenin, stand accused of denying 'life itself'. In Anna and her husband, Tolstoy is stating the paradox that we should be incautious—and afraid.

Karenin may not be 'felt', he may not have fair treatment, but in some ways he is very close to Tolstoy. He is Tolstoy's pet hate, a living index of all that Tolstoy loathes—bureaucracy, self-importance, coldness and calculation. Tolstoy's faith in the natural man, the noble savage, may at times strike us as ingenuous. The case for this is most strongly presented in Levin, who, like Tolstoy, rejects and despises officialdom. Levin is no less irrational than Anna is. This does not prevent his enjoying a special dispensation; Levin can do no wrong in Tolstoy's eyes. But even Levin is not exempt from the method employed by Tolstoy, the device, which partly makes the book so real, of showing us the characters as they appear to each other. Just as we may ourselves in life have friends whom we recognise would not get on, whose incompatibility does not alter our affection for them, but does give us a sense of seeing them in a context, of seeing them as they cannot see themselves—so, committed to Levin, we first view Vronsky through his eyes. Later, however, we cannot deny the justice of Vronsky's reaction to Levin. We do not share Anna's triumph at the ball; we witness it as spectators, in this way far more sharply, looking on through Kitty's tortured gaze. By this device we are made to see people in the round, to see, as it were, the obverse side of the coin. Karenin alone is denied the benefit of this method. He is, none the less, the product of it. Karenin, with his denial of life, is surely nothing other than the obverse side of Anna's coin.

Viewed in this way as a figure put together from qualities which are simply the opposite of Anna's, Karenin, it
seems to me, becomes explicable. Much of our confusion
falls away. But what, as the critical reader must already
have detected, emerges is not, in fact, a clarity, but merely
a clarification, a clearer apprehension of what is really the
cause of our confusion. As must appear most flagrantly
in the case of Karenin, my analysis implies a duality. It is
itself contradictory. On the one hand, I have said, there
are the facts, facts which by no means constitute an indictment of Karenin, which show him indeed as far from being
unfeeling. On the other hand there is Tolstoy's presentation of him—cold, ambitious, a typical bureaucrat.

It is not without interest to compare Karenin alone,
left to Tolstoy's none too tender mercies, as in the chapter
in which he considers the respective merits of a duel,
divorce or separation, and Karenin when we see him
together with other persons. Thus, when Anna makes her
confession to him, he feels compassion for her and masters
himself by an effort. A moment later he is alone in the
carriage tucking the rug round his knees like an old
woman. And now, we are informed, his only thought is
how best to shake off the mud she has spattered him with
in her fall. He ponders and rejects all three courses, in
favour of preserving a nominal *status quo*, on condition
that Anna breaks with Vronsky. Having reached this conclusion, a further consideration now adds its weight to
these others for him. ' "That is the only course in keeping
with . . . religion" ', he told himself. In adopting this
solution he is not merely casting off a guilty wife, but
giving her a chance to mend her ways. And however hard

it may be for him he will devote himself to her reforma-
tion and salvation. 'Though in . . . these painful moments'
Karenin 'had not once thought of seeking guidance in
religion . . . this religious sanction . . . afforded him . . .
satisfaction.' It pleased him that even in such a crisis as
this, no one could accuse him of not acting 'in accordance
with . . . that religion whose standard he had always held
aloft'. Of course she will not be happy, 'but I am not to
blame, and so I cannot be unhappy'.

On this complacent note, the journey at an end, we
retire with Karenin to his study. ' "I will see no one", he
instructs the porter, accentuating with a certain pleasure
the words "see no one." It was a sign that he was in a
good temper.'

We witness his self-satisfaction as, without once hesita-
ting, he proceeds to compose his letter to Anna, announcing his decision and requesting her return. Having
finished the letter, folded it, 'smoothed it with a massive
ivory paper-knife and put it in an envelope, he rang . . .
with the gratification the use of his well-arranged writing
materials always aroused in him'.

For sheer spite and malice this would be hard to beat.
Yet there are times when he is made deeply moving, as on
the occasion of his tête-à-tête with Dolly:

' "But what has she done?" asked Dolly.

' "She has treated her duty with contempt and betrayed
her husband. That is what she has done," he said.

' "No, no, it can't be! Don't say that, for God's sake;
you must be mistaken," Dolly exclaimed. . . .

'Karenin smiled coldly merely with his lips, meaning
to signify to her and to himself the firmness of his con-

viction; but this passionate defence of Anna though it did not shake him, reopened his wound. He began to speak with greater heat.

' "It is extremely difficult to be mistaken when a wife informs her husband herself—informs him that eight years of married life and a son have all been an error, and that she wants to begin life again," he said angrily, with a snort.

' "Anna and transgression—I cannot connect the two. . . !"

' "Darya Alexandrovna", he said, now looking straight into Dolly's kind, troubled face . . . "I would give a great deal still to be able to have any doubts. While I was in doubt I was miserable, but it was not so bad as it is now. When I doubted I could hope, but now there is no hope, and still I doubt everything. I am in such doubt of everything I cannot bear my son, and sometimes do not believe he is my son. I am very unhappy."

'He had no need to say that. Dolly had seen it as soon as he glanced into her face; and she felt sorry for him, and her faith in her friend's innocence began to totter.

' "Oh this is awful, awful! But can it be true that you are resolved on a divorce?" '

One cannot, Karenin says, go on living *à trois*.

' "I understand, I quite understand that. . . . But wait! You are a Christian! Think of her! What will become of her if you cast her off?"

' "I have thought, Darya Alexandrovna. I have thought a great deal", said Karenin. His face became mottled and his dim eyes looked straight into hers. Dolly at that moment pitied him with all her heart. "I did that very

thing when she herself informed me of my humiliation. I
left everything as of old. I gave her a chance to reform.
I tried to save her. And with what result? She would not
heed the easiest of demands—that she should observe the
proprieties," he went on, getting heated. "You can only
save a person who wants to be saved. But if the whole
nature is so corrupt, so depraved, that ruin itself seems
to her salvation, what can one do?" '

It is impossible, I think, not to feel Dolly here as a
corrective to Tolstoy's attitude. Her presence makes it
impossible for Tolstoy to indulge his usual implacable
hatred for Karenin. Karenin's words have a justice. We
too, no less than Dolly, pity him from the bottom of our
hearts.

Reading, re-reading the book we have a growing sense
of the shadow-play of Tolstoy's own feelings. Viewing
the characters as we do through each other's eyes, we
frequently have the sensation of a time-lag; as if, leaving
one for another, Tolstoy had dropped behind, had failed
to make the necessary transition. At such moments we
have, as it were, a glimpse of Tolstoy's coat-tails whisking
round the corner out of sight, as he slides noiselessly into
place behind Levin or Vronsky. Where Karenin is concerned he is less discreet. Too often, forgetting his
author's role, he steps from behind the screen and looms
before us shaking a wrathful fist.

As I have said we are carried along on the tide of
Tolstoy's feelings. We do not doubt that Karenin is
repellent. Only on close inspection, and with some amaze-
ment, do we perceive that he is not a monster. The facts

and the presentation cannot be made to tally. And yet—this too is a fact we have to face—one man is the author of both. Tolstoy's detestation of Karenin does not make him leave out the facts, does not, in other words, lead him to create Karenin differently. Similarly with Anna, Tolstoy's sympathy for her obscures but does not exclude her weaknesses.

'Tolstoy', says Professor Christian, 'does not judge Anna.' This is true. The anomaly remains. Tolstoy has preferences. We do not doubt that Levin is his favourite. Vronsky earns our respect, the more so let us observe, since we feel that Tolstoy is hard on him.

In other words Anna, Vronsky and Levin lead their own lives independently of their creator. But no, this is not quite it. They go their own ways but with Tolstoy's agreement that they do so. He agrees to this in the interests of truth. His features, the old prejudices are there, but chastened and subdued, invested with a demureness that cannot fail at times to raise a smile. Aha! we think, so you're here! Served up in this quiet manner his quirks and kinks are not unpalatable. As for Tolstoy's feelings for his characters, his favouritism, his arbitrary loves and hates—on analysis, it is true, these seemed to cloud his meaning, as in Anna's relation with Karenin. Now we see that this counter-current even is pressed into service, these feelings too, subserve Tolstoy's end. They prove his characters real. It is through his relation with them that we share their reality for Tolstoy.

The overlapping method so effectively used by Tolstoy to depict his characters in the round—thus we know that

Levin is real, since we constantly see him reflected in different ways through different people's eyes—serves curiously both to connect and also to dissever. Architectonically it interlocks. In Tolstoy's two themes we have two disparate worlds. Anna's world is night, Levin's day. Matter and style are poles apart, so far apart indeed that their very contrast spins the plot. Thus we have Levin returning from Moscow, sad and humiliated after his proposal and rejection. Met by Ignat, the coachman, riding along in his own upholstered sledge, watching his horses with plaited tails and the harness with rings and tassels, his mind occupied with village news, Levin 'felt himself and did not want to be anyone else'. Whereas Anna seated in the train asks herself: "'Who am I, myself or someone else?'" The two episodes are complementary. Similarly we invariably proceed from heights to depths and vice versa, from Vronsky's high spirits to Kitty's depression and illness, from Anna's broken marriage to Levin's longing for the married state. During the very dinner-party in the course of which Karenin retires with Dolly to the nursery, while he is explaining to her his reasons for divorce, Levin is becoming engaged to Kitty.

Structurally, this connects. Personally, the effect is to stress the characters' isolation. Critics are oddly neglectful of the extraordinary passage in which Anna becomes Vronsky's mistress. Stylistically even Tolstoy loses all control. The writing is as rabid, as venomous as if he were himself tearing love to pieces. 'Vronsky felt what a murderer must feel when he looks at the body he has robbed of life. . . . But in spite of the murderer's horror before the body of his victim, that body must be hacked

to pieces and hidden, and the murderer must make use of
what he has obtained by his crime.

'And, as with fury and passion the murderer throws
himself upon the body and drags it and hacks at it, so he
covered her face and shoulders with kisses. . . . The body
he had robbed of life was their love, the first stage of their
love. . . .'

Anna does not pause to consider Vronsky's feelings.
She does not conceal her disgust and humiliation. She is
crouching on the floor, grovelling at his feet. 'At last,
as though making an effort over herself, she sat up and
pushed him away.

' "Everything is over," she said. "I have nothing but
you left. Remember that."

' "I can never forget what is life itself to me. For one
moment of happiness like this. . . ."

' "Happiness!" she said with disgust and horror and
her horror was involuntarily communicated to him. "For
pity's sake do not speak of it—do not speak of it
again. . . ."

' "Do not speak of it," she repeated and with a look of
cold despair, incomprehensible to him, she left him.'

Love itself divides, serves only to isolate.

Later it will be Vronsky who recoils, whose turn it is
to be physically repelled by Anna's love. ' "My desire
arouses his disgust," Anna thinks in the carriage. "Don't
I know . . . that he won't be unfaithful to me? I know all
that, but it doesn't make it any the easier for me. If he does
not love me, but treats me kindly and gently out of a
sense of *duty*, and what I want is not there—that would
be a thousand times worse than . . . hate. . . . It would be

hell. And that is just how it is. He has long ceased to love me. And where love ends, hate begins." '

It is indeed hard to say where the line is drawn. Loathing is there at the heart of love. Tolstoy could never obliterate the sense of his child-bride's terror; his horror of performing the sexual act with a sheltered pure young girl of his own social class long outlived revulsion on Sonya's side. It is easy to vilify Tolstoy's attitude to love. It seems to us monstrous, because abnormal. But in a sense he is merely rejecting Victorian morals, recoiling— this is too easily overlaid by the hugely powerful image of him imprinted on our minds—with a sensitiveness, a sensibility quite as painfully acute, no less than that of Keats. The wonder is that this sensitivity, combined with Tolstoy's idealisation of his dead mother, did not succeed in making him impotent. And the tragedy is perhaps that he did not marry Aksynia, a wife such as Cézanne's wife, or a Madame Renoir.

Vronsky's love for her cannot cure Anna's isolation. He is all that is left to her in life. If unwisely, it is scarcely surprising that she clutches at him—and if Vronsky asserts his independence. 'Where love ends, hate begins.' In the end it is perhaps true to say that the two are indivisible. 'Then she thought . . . how wretchedly she loved and hated him, and how violently her heart was beating.'

To read this sentence is to feel Anna's heart still beating, throbbing like a bird between our hands. Will she, may she not even now escape? Yes, even now perhaps she might have done so, had it not been for Dolly's failure to understand her; to Dolly she is merely not herself. ' "Yes there was something peculiar about her today", said Dolly. Dolly had "almost fancied" she was crying.'

In the last resort her derangement is due to isolation. Driving away from Dolly's, she sees two men: what can the one be telling the other with such ardour? ' "Can one ever tell anyone what one is feeling?" ' We watch her receding each moment further out of reach. On her fatal journey to the station she sees a shop sign: ' "Tuitkin Coiffeur, Je me fais Coiffer par Tuitkin". "I'll tell him that when he comes home," she thought and smiled. But then she remembered that she had no one now to tell funny things to. "Besides there's nothing funny, nothing amusing really. Everything's hateful. . . . Why these churches, the bells, the humbug? To hide the fact that we all hate each other. . . ." ' What is so familiar about this to us? What does it remind us of? Yes, of course we know. This is the wild utterance of Ophelia.

And only now do we recognise the meaning of Anna's 'radiance'. Let us look back and consider the references to it. It is there when we and Vronsky first meet her on the train. . . . 'The uncontrollable radiance of her eyes and her smile set him [Vronsky] on fire', when she leaves the ball. In the fever induced by the heat in the railway carriage 'a red light blinded her eyes'. When she enters the bedroom with Karenin 'the fire in her now seemed quenched or hidden far away'. Returning to face her husband in her boudoir, 'Anna walked in with bent head, playing with the tassels of her hood. Her face shone with a vivid glow; but it was not a joyous glow—it suggested the terrible glow of a fire on a dark night. On seeing her husband,

Anna raised her head and smiled, as if waking from a dream.' Memories of her last meeting with Vronsky 'fire her blood. "Heavens how light it is!"' she exclaims. '"It's dreadful but I do love to see his face and I do love this fantastic light." ' Later we see her meditating an overdose of opium; she is staring at the 'cornice of the ceiling and the shadow the screen cast on it. . . . Suddenly the shadow of the screen wavered, pounced on the whole cornice, the whole ceiling.' Other shadows 'darted across to meet it'. The candle has gone out. The room is plunged in darkness. ' "Death!" she thought. And such horror fell upon her that for a long while she could not make out where she was, and her trembling hands could not find a match. . . .' ' "And now," ' as she drives away from Dolly's in the carriage, 'and now for the first time Anna turned the glaring light in which she was seeing everything upon her relations with him. . . . "Why not put out the candle when there's nothing more to see, when everything looks obnoxious?" ' she asks herself. All this, the final paragraph, the snuffing of the candle by which she has been reading the book of life, the last brilliant flaring up of that candle which illumined 'all that before had been enshrouded in darkness . . . before it finally flickered, grew dim and went out for ever'—this is unfashionably obvious stuff today. The metaphor embarrasses our 'subtler' modern ear. His symbols, we are told, are 'inherently clumsy'. 'Tolstoy's symbolic touch is far from delicate'—so we are told by Mr John Bayley.[1] This seems to me rather a question of taste—of fashion, of era. If Tolstoy's symbols seem hackneyed to us today, we cannot, wish as we may to do so,

[1] *Tolstoy and the Novel*, p. 216.

disclaim the palpable fact that we ourselves belong to a
generation perfectly happy to sit out the certainly no less
banal, portentous symbols of Antonioni. We may, surely,
as well deplore George Eliot's 'sentiment'. Possibly, as
Professor Christian puts it, the game of hunt-the-symbol
is best played with other authors.[1] The flames which
devour Anna are real enough—they are the fire of love,
and, too, the fire of hell, the hellish radiance of an inner
world, which blinds one to the features of external reality
and finally claims Anna for its own.

Yet it is love that saves Levin from his own despair.
But it is love, too, that drives him to it. Love, his love for
Kitty, married happiness, cannot free Levin from thoughts
of suicide, any more than illicit love can satisfy Anna.
Love cannot solve the enigma of death, cannot remove
the fact that we must 'perish miserably'. Significantly one
chapter in the book only has a title—this is headed
'Death'. Both Tolstoy's chief protagonists are led by very
different routes to the same objective—death. And there
is a glancing meeting-point, a point at which Levin does
draw very near to Anna: ' "I cannot live without knowing
what I am. And that I can't know. . . ." Levin would say
to himself. . . . This was an agonising fallacy. . . . But it was
not only fallacy, it was the cruel jest of some evil power,
some evil inimical power to which one could not submit.

'He must escape from this power. And each man held
the means of escape in his own hands. An end *must* be put
to this dependence on evil. And there was one means—
death.'

[1] *Tolstoy: A Critical Introduction*, Cambridge University Press
(my italics), p. 207.

A DARING COIFFEUR

To Anna also life is simply a malignant jest. ' "Are we not all flung into the world for no other purpose than to hate each other, and so to torture ourselves and one another?" '

Anna hurls her death not only as she has thrown her love, like a missile, in Vronsky's teeth; she throws it in the teeth of life, of fate, of God. Momentarily these two paths overlap. Levin has none of Anna's motives, he has no self-pity; he has no desire to hit his wife. He merely wishes to free himself from a wrong relation, not with Kitty but with life itself. But—this is the point; that here there *exists* a relationship. Levin is kept alive, if in despair, by ties, by his sense of duty, his obligations to others. The answer resides in what he has always known. It is the same answer as when he took part in the mowing. Just as then when the scythe seemed to mow of itself, when he ceased to be conscious of what he was doing and then he did it well— 'these', says Tolstoy, 'were the most blessed moments'— so now, when he ceases to look for reasons, he knows instinctively what he should do and what he should not do.

But reason was given us as a means to escape from our troubles, says Anna, echoing the woman in the train. The reader is moved when she says this since, as he knows, Anna has never been accessible to reason. She clutches now at this thought because it fits her mood. She has never, in fact, been more remote from reason. And, this being so, we may well feel Tolstoy is making use of this passage, the woman in the train, to discredit reason. Levin himself rejects it; it is intellectual pride. He does not appear to have heard of spiritual pride. He does not, it seems, distinguish between what one knows to be right, and what may, after all, be mere self-will. Despite his rejection of it, Levin is, in fact, himself using reason to escape from doubt, from what it is impossible to know. Faith in what he knows to be right or wrong, in its instinctive finite sense, is not sufficient for him. Levin needs and indeed creates a dogma. He comes to us—alas!—hot-foot with a message, the message of Tolstoy's new-found religious faith.

In the apiary he welcomes the chance to be alone. Just as the bees buzzing and circling around him threaten him physically, so life's 'petty cares' had restricted Levin's 'spiritual freedom'.

Already we see Tolstoy moving into the distance, opting for the ultimate isolation.

And sadly we feel that it was perhaps always bound to be so. We reflect upon the mystery of his art. Was it not, after all, always incipiently anti-art? We remember Levin in the wood, his surliness in response to Koznyshev's raptures. 'Levin,' we remember that we were told, 'did not like talking or hearing about the beauty of nature. *Words for him detracted from the beauty of what he saw.*' [1] We recall the peculiarity of Tolstoy's relation with language. It is as if he has taken a short cut. And so in a sense he has—a short cut via Pushkin, who purged Russian literature of rhetoric. Tolstoy's admitted aim was to write of the inner world as clearly as Pushkin wrote of the outer one; to move from simple narrative, carrying that simplicity into the complex world of motivation. In some ways Tolstoy strikes us as curiously miscast, an odd protagonist of the inner world, designed surely by nature

[1] My italics.

as the property of life, life in its most extroverted sense. He is singularly lacking in the appurtenances of the aesthete, or even, indeed, of the literary man. Possibly, *Childhood, Boyhood and Youth* suggests, we owe Tolstoy primarily to his painful self-consciousness. The agonies for him of youth engendered the early habit of lacerating self-analysis. Without this habit and outlook already established manhood with its sensuality might not have produced the tragic division in him. Without it we might not have had the author. We could not have had the author of *Childhood, Boyhood and Youth*, with its apparently effortless early style. But this is the point—it is not an introverted style. It does not grope confusedly for truth. It is limpidly clear, as crystalline as if there were nothing uncertain, as if we were still dealing with externals, as if, in other words, there were nothing to analyse. This written style connects with his view of truth. Truth, for him, has nothing to do with words, with accuracy. It would still be there without the words. Admittedly he re-wrote, corrected endlessly. But somehow, almost surely deliberately, he neglected to tidy up, to delete the repetitions. He thus preserved a freshness of expression that carries a peculiarly disarming, artless ring. Tolstoy was never embroiled, locked with language. At times his innocence goes so far as to make him amateurish. Writing of Anna's seduction at Vronsky's hands, he seems, as I have remarked, to lose all control. In his preface to *Childhood, Boyhood and Youth*, Tolstoy delineates the readers he is addressing: 'persons who instinctively understand him . . . who need not have my feelings and inclinations explained. One need not explain or expound

anything to them. But may,' he says, 'with full confidence'
pass on to these initiates 'ideas very vaguely expressed.
There are delicate, intangible relations between feelings
for which there exists no clear expression.'

Tolstoy is here denying the usefulness of language. He
is not, like other serious writers, concerned to forge a
language that will bear his meaning. The effort is to come
from the reader's side. And that reader is to be—sympathetic to Tolstoy!

As I have said his attitude to language is, I think,
closely related to his conception of truth. Let us return
to the preface from which I have quoted. 'Truth', says
Tolstoy, 'comes from the heart and not the head.' Once
more we are back with Levin, the noble savage. 'When
you write from the head the words arrange themselves
obediently and fluently on the paper. But when you write
from the heart so many thoughts crowd in . . ., so many
images . . . , so many memories . . . , that the expression',
says Tolstoy, 'becomes inexact, inadequate, intractable
and rough.'

We may feel Pushkin's influence, the limpid narrative
style imposed by Tolstoy on matter far from clear, contributed to his attitude and ultimately produced his
damagingly simple view of truth. We may remember
Levin's 'clever' remark at Anna's. The talk has turned on
the new French realist school, which is attacked for taking
realism to the point of coarseness. Levin defends the
French for whom, he says, having carried conventionality
further than anyone else, the new trend is a natural healthy
one. 'The French', says Levin, 'saw poetry in the fact
of not lying.' Once again we glimpse Tolstoy's coat-tails.

'No clever remark,' we read, 'uttered by Levin had ever given him so much satisfaction as this one.'

We take our leave of Tolstoy under the stars with Levin. Suddenly Levin hears Kitty's voice: ' "You're not upset about anything are you?" she inquired peering intently into his face in the starlight.'

She could not have seen his expression had not a flash of lightning, blotting out the stars, illumined it.

' "She understands," he thought. [He is thinking of his faith]. "Shall I tell her or not? Yes, I will. . . ."

'But just as he opened his mouth to speak she turned to him first.

' "Oh Kostya, be nice and go and see if Sergei Ivanitch will be comfortable in the corner-room. . . . See if they've put the new wash-stand in."

' "Very well, I'll go directly," said Levin . . . kissing her.

' "No, I had better not speak of it," he thought. "It is a secret for me alone, of vital importance for me, *and not to be put into words.*" ' [1]

[1] My italics.